I0203459

Sweetly Alive

Poetry Books by Anna Grossnickle Hines

Peaceful Pieces: Quilts and Poems about Peace
Winter Lights: A Season in Poems and Quilts
Pieces: A Year in Poems and Quilts

Enhanced iBook by the Morning Call Poets

Poems of Joy from On the Call

Sweetly Alive

POEMS

ANNA GROSSNICKLE HINES

APPROPO
2015

Copyright © 2015 by Anna Grossnickle Hines

All rights reserved.

First Printing: 2015

ISBN 978-1-938771-01-9

appropo llc
P.O. Box 1456
Gualala, California, 95445

appropo.co@gmail.com

www.appropo.co

For my dear friends
on the Morning Call—
Andrea, Jeffery, Mary Beth, Denise,
Lisa, Diane, Vera, and Peggy D.—
and for our mentor, Peggy Rubin,
and all those who join
and support us in creating
a force field for joy.

ACKNOWLEDGEMENTS

A special thank you to Lisa Nelson, Mary Beth Watt, Andrea Wachter, and my daughter, Sarah Hines Stephens, for their editorial skills and encouragement, to my husband Gary for his unfailing support, to Timmie Tanyakul for her spiritual guidance, and to my family from whom I continue to learn so much about love.

Contents

The Morning Call

Nature as Sacred

Exploring the Mystery

Seeking Purpose

Being Love

Connection and Change

I have nothing new to say
but still this poetry arises in me
like the tremble of an old drum
struck again by the player's hand.
                    ~B.T. Joy

My Journey

Most mornings I keep an eye on the clock, not wanting to be late for my Morning Call. Cup of tea beside me and the poem for the day on my computer or iPad screen, I push the numbers on the phone and join my group of friends. We check in, discuss the weather and life's events, as we wait for others to join. Then the poem is read by the one whose turn it was to choose. We listen as she reads and after a few quiet moments for pondering, begin to share, reflecting the poem's meaning and connections in our lives and on our journey together. Often one of us has written a poem in response, and we reflect on that as well, before signing off with our own version of the Ho'oponopono Prayer and "Peace is on my heart and on the earth," in five languages.

My home is in the redwoods, just a mile from the Pacific Ocean, near the tiny town of Gualala, California, a most beautiful and peaceful place. I love to share it with family and friends, when they can come, but mostly it is just my husband, myself, and our border collie, Tucker. After raising three daughters, and a long career writing and illustrating children's books—several of the last ones being poetry illustrated with quilts—and a stab at creating picture book apps, I now see my spiritual journey as primary. It is my task to live with awareness in the sacredness of life itself.

As for so many others, my childhood was not without troubles, mainly my father's seemingly unpredictable and terrifying temper, and my parents' repeated separations and eventual divorce. As the oldest in a large family I felt a lot of responsibility to care for my mother and siblings and it was often painful. Fortunately, I believed the words I learned in Sunday school, that God is Love. I knew I was a good girl and I knew that a loving God would not punish me, so I surmised that I was being prepared for important work. God needed me to be strong. I had a sense of myself surrounded by an all-encompassing Love.

Even then I saw the world in an inclusive, holistic way, and much of life made little sense to me. Why were the colors on the maps different for the different countries when the plants and trees were green everywhere? Why was I asked to pledge allegiance to the flag and people of this country when people everywhere had the same needs for food, safety, and love? What did the term "good God-fearing people" mean? Why would *good* people need to fear God? Why would God choose one group of people to know the truth and leave others out? Was it a loving act to destroy the culture of another group to spread the idea of God's love? How could there be wars in God's name? That wasn't the God I knew, the God I felt around me.

By the time I was in high school, though I loved the community singing and friends I made in church, I wasn't finding God there. For me God was not a super-natural being at all, not a great male Father-in-Heaven, but an essence, a wisdom that was in all things, including me. To know God, all I had to do was to go to that place in me, a place that was easier to find in nature than a building. I stopped calling whatever that essence was God, a word too entangled with negative implications, but didn't know any other name to use.

A year out of high school, I married a man who turned out to be even more erratic and far less responsible than my father, giving me lots more opportunity to be made strong for that purpose for which I still sensed I was intended. On my own with two children I returned to college, Pacific Oaks, a school founded by Quakers, which had a strong focus on personal development. I studied Human Development; Third Force Psychology (the psychology of health rather than disease), Carl Jung, Abraham Maslow, Carl Rogers, theories of creativity and full human potential. Then came a wiser marriage, the years focused on building and raising my family, and the career of my dreams, challenging and rewarding years. Was this it? Was this my purpose? The children? The books? Always I was reading and exploring, seeking that deeper experience, and wondering when I would know…if I would know.

Soon after I turned fifty my last child left home, my career faltered, and the questions came back more intensely. I read Carolyn Myss, Deepak Chopra, Joseph Campbell, Shirley MacLaine, Gary Zukav, Eckhardt Tolle, Thich Nhat Hanh and others. I made attempts at meditating. I talked with friends who had some of the same questions. What was this purpose? Was I doing it? At the turn of the century I met a new friend and teacher, Timmie Tanyakul, who told me I had gotten a little lost and she was supposed to help me get back on track. I learned much from her, how to let go of some things, trust the Divine within more fully, to know that I was, in essence, that Divine, and that I did indeed have work to do. Eckhardt Tolle wrote of those who are meant to hold a frequency. His words ring true. I believe that is my task.

In 2010, distracted by so many disturbing world events, struggling to keep my balance in holding the frequency and sending blessings, I signed up for Jean Houston's year long *Mystery School: Spiritual Life in Tumultuous Times*. Jean's lectures were inspiring and the readings wonderful, harking back to my studies at Pacific Oaks and tying in new learnings and developments that had come about in the years since. Particularly exciting were the discoveries in quantum physics and molecular biology that were seeming to support or parallel spiritual thought.

For me, though, the most valuable gift of the course was the birth of the Morning Call. We were assigned a daily reading, provided by Jean's teaching partner, Peggy Rubin, and several of us decided to share the experience on a morning conference call. Many of us wrote poems in response, almost daily.

Some of us had written poems before, but others had not. Peggy was so delighted with what we were doing, that the following year she collected our writings together and gave them back to us in her *Year for Joy*, a calendar with one of our own poems to be read each day for the next year.

In her introduction Peggy Rubin wrote:

> Much misery pervades the earth, and the time has come to lift it off somewhat, so that life can move and breathe more freely. One way is for you to become a force field for joy.
>
> Your own sense of buoyant joy comes first; otherwise you will not find the strength to do this work. Nor will you realize the essential truth that joy is the primary element in all creation until you recognize yourself as an energy being of purest joy.
>
> How do you get there? Practice. Practice. Practice.

And so we practice. When the second year was over, we chose to take turns selecting the poems, sometimes our own, but more often the poetry of others, searching books and the internet to find the poems and poets who spoke to us, enjoying our discoveries. We post these not only for one another, but on a listserve for Jean's past Mystery School students, and her Social Artistry Foundation. For the past three years we have also participated in Peggy's Evolutionary Journey Workshop with its focus on establishing community and awakening the Goddess energy within ourselves and the world. We often contribute and share our writings with that group as well.

We live in Chicago, Connecticut, California, and Oregon, so for some it is a Noontime or late Morning Call. A few who began with us have dropped and others have joined. Andrea Wachter, Denise Dignan, Mary Beth Watt, Jeffery Baker, Lisa Nelson, Vera Grant, Diane Dwyer, and myself are now in our sixth year of this practice. Ramapriya Ruiz was with us until her passing in 2012, and Peggy Dean joined us a couple years ago. Each of us has expressed that this Call has become essential for her. Not all of us are on every day, but several are, and even on those very rare times when it is just one, she still reads the poem aloud. We hate to miss, for it *is* a practice, a touching in to what sustains us in maintaining the focus on joy, purpose, and spirit.

As I sorted through our writings earlier this year, it seemed to me it was time to put some of the poems I have created through this practice into a book to be shared. I hope you will find poems here that speak to you, that call out your joy, help you connect with your own purpose, your own community, and add to that great force field so needed in our world.

Please, pour yourself a nice cup of tea, take a quiet moment, and join me on the Call.

The Morning Call

THE MORNING FIRE CIRCLE

Waking in the predawn light
I look out at the last stars
twinkling in my circle of sky above the trees.
I stretch and put my kettle on
knowing others in my circle also stir,
do morning rituals.
Those in the east have already
had their morning tea or coffee,
eaten their oatmeal or toast and eggs,
and are well into their day,
but soon…soon…we will gather,
ears to our phones,
eyes on the words of today's
inspirational writing.
We will circle round to tell our stories,
stoke the fires of our understanding,
our connection,
the growing glow dispersing fears,
spreading compassion,
giving light to our vision
of a world joyfully ablaze in love.

DOING THE WORK

Each day I intend
       to do more exercise
       write more praise songs
       do more drawing
       eat less sugar
       tend my roses
       take more deep breaths
       make more phone calls
       sit by the pond
       walk the labyrinth
       do more reading
       and more dancing
       and more singing.
Each day I intend
       not all, but some,
       some each day
but the hours slip by
       and it is evening
       and I sit
       holding my intentions
except this one
       this one I keep
       to dial the numbers
       read or listen to the daily poem
       reflect, laugh, empathize
       join for these moments each day
       everyday
renewing my vows to be grateful
       to be loving
       to hold peace in my heart
       and on the earth
       and it is enough
enough to carry that thread
       that carries me through
       whatever else happens
       in my days.

FROM THE QUILTER

Denise's mythical musical connections,
dancing with celestial bodies,
Andrea's ties to mother,
earth and goddess,
Mary Beth's clear-sighted vision,
nature and spirit closely entwined,
Dawn rescuer, receiver,
teller of stories deep and true,
Jeffery's link to place and space,
inner and outer, a calm connection,
Ramapriya's porous membranes,
opening channels with rhythm and sound,
Osha's excitability, brightness shining,
magical twinkling woman-child,
Vera's depth of listening, questioning,
bringing focus, words of wisdom,
The poetry and voices of others,
charging and sparking each morning call,
emerging from Peggy's vision of joy.
How important—how essential—
you have all become
to my every day.

THE FLAME

Some mornings my candle
feels a bit lonely
but then the glow illuminates
the place where we connect
and together dance
in the ever widening circle.

Gray Morning

At first glance this morning
my sky is a solid gray,
no identifying features,
a solid canopy lighting my world of trees
and greens and blooming plants.
Looking closer,
brighter patches and wisps of darker ones
begin to define themselves.
Reading the words of my friend brings chills;
her encompassing of the pains and joys
within the same circle,
in the same breath,
takes mine away,
as overhead my sky grows more mottled
with lights and darks,
joy and pain intermingling,
and I breathe in my own appreciation
of the nuances.

Morning Call

A black cat
a small white dog
doors opening into gardens
fresh morning air
the daily walk
the call of the crow
reflections on dreams
moments of silence shared
words pensive
or celebratory
encouraging
opening
calling me out
into each joy filled day.

RESPONDING TO THE POET'S CALL

The morning conversation
calling into form
journeys into and out of misty vistas,
poetry as contagious,
the history of cursive writing
back through the ages,
through scribes of ancient tomes,
elaborate and elegant,
to the cave paintings
calling forth the life in stone,
the flow,
rhythm and movement,
large and small,
releasing the hidden into form
and we wonder,
as old forms are lost,
what new may emerge
once again from the mist?

Go out…
go out, as the poet says,
and shout it from your belly,
wave your arms in wide and flowing circles,
draw the images,
write the words in flourishes upon the sky,
whatever it is,
the new…
the emerging…
the contagious joy…
bring it into being,
let it flow
from the always mysterious mist.

On Mother's Day

We are daughters of the earth
mothered, smothered,
neglected, grown,
finding our way,
filling the gaps,
mothering our own
and one another,
nurturing the earth,
pregnant now
with possibilities of what will be.
I thank you, my sisters,
my mothers of the soul
as we share
in pain and ecstasy
this labor for the birth.

Thank You, Lisa and Denise

Rereading your poems
I look over the top of my computer
to the fog
drifting down over the redwoods,
and the raptor
dark wings spread
circling...
circling...
circling...

I too forget the chores
the lists
the unmade bed
to become
in this moment
pure joy.

Peeling the Layers

On the night of the full moon
my people loving dog
snarls and snaps.
I don't understand.
For love he returns this?
Lying restless under the moon's bright light
I struggle against the pull into darkness.
What have I done?
How can I fix it?

Today the poem speaks of the soul's dark energy.
I trust the poet,
but her words have a strange resonance,
Radiate darkness?
Isn't it my work to spread the light?
Speaking to me on that deep level,
down in the dark where I went last night,
her words rattle my bones, shake me up,
but I'm not clear, not clear, not clear.

On the morning call I hear talk
of the fecundity of the darkness,
of the ever-present mystery,
of cycles ever bigger,
circles with no beginning and no end,
or rather, each moment being both
the end and the beginning.

Listening to the voices
with my heart broken open
the words begin to come…
Accept this moment.
Accept this moment.
Each is its own revelation.
Peeling back the layers of the mystery
reveals more mystery.
Peel and accept,
cycles within cycles.

Move back and see the big picture.
It is a dance,
moments of darkness,
moments of clarity.

Accept this moment.
Let go of judgment.
Let go of the need to understand.
Let go of the need to fix,
to make everything light,
to make everything clear.
Love without need for response,
without expectation,
without condition.
Accept this moment.
It's part of the dance.

SUNRISE IN GUALALA

The rising sun
sends glittering rainbow rays
through openings
in the dense redwoods.
Glowing white
clouds float above the
white-cloud-pear-trees
and calla lilies
and lush new growth of spring
as I read a message of
sunset on Moloka'i
and anticipate shared voices
shared quiet
in communion
on the morning call,
our hearts
singing in unison.

THANKS FOR THE REMINDER

Scrambling with the morning emails
thank yous and corrections,
and news to share,
comments to the White House on climate change,
I pause as the sun peaks over the top of my computer.
Through the redwoods
it's brilliant center
haloed by rainbow rays
reaches out to me
reaches out in all directions.
I stop to read the morning poem
and am reminded by my friend
of the true work,
the world changing work.
I light my candle and look into the flame,
holding with her
a vision of the change,
allowing it to expand in my heart,
to send out the sparkling rainbow rays,
like the sun,
like the candle,
like the poem,
doing the work.

Bags Packed and Ready

The time draws near.
Today I'll pack my bag.
My daughter wants me there for the birth,
for her first days as a mother,
as I was with her sisters,
watching them hold their newborns,
witness to the breaking open of their hearts
to a love more fierce than they knew was possible,
as mine echoed, remembering
and breaking open once again to this new joy.
They don't really need me.
They have the instincts and their hearts
to guide them,
but how nice to be wanted,
how thrilling to be in this circle of love,
of renewal.

Each morning
on the call with my friends
there is a bit of that,
a bit of the breaking open
as we birth joy over and over,
sharing, connecting, remembering, awakening
a sense of wonder, renewal, possibility.
I sleep each night with my bags packed,
ready for the journey,
ready to be mother, midwife, sister, lover
as we venture together
into each new day.

MEETING ON THE MOUNTAINTOP

We go through our days,
each meeting her challenges,
her joys,
her moments of agony,
of numbness,
of passionate creativity,
sometimes sure-footed,
sometimes stumbling.
Each of us,
individually.
But each morning
at this appointed hour,
we open our hearts,
and together climb
to this high place,
where agonies,
and joys are shared,
where our best and
most heart-felt intentions
are expressed, examined,
multiplied ten-fold, a hundred-fold,
lifting, enlightening, enfolding each
and all of us
that we may then
go through our days,
our passions and challenges,
standing more solidly
on this higher ground.

To Ramapriya

I spoke of you today
with your luminous snowy hair
and eyes on fire.
I spoke of you,
of your rhythms and melodies
beating their patterns,
creating an ambience,
filling rooms.
I spoke of you,
of your passion to reach out,
bring in, extend, lift up,
invite into the dance,
to include all in the one.
I spoke of you,
your smile,
your laugh.
I hold you in this moment
so happy to have been touched
by your miraculousness,
and when too soon you have gone,
I will hold this love,
this vision of your eyes on fire,
your grace in angelic form
dancing in the light,
showing me the way.

GIVE US THIS DAY

Drawn back day after day
to this morning dose of poetry
laughter, spiritual camaraderie,
I get a glimpse of why
the devout go to daily mass.
I am tempted to say
it grounds me
but that seems too earthy a phrase.

Tethers might be a better choice;
tethers me to my place in the matrix
which is no place and every place,
stirs my awareness of being
in the vast field where everything is possible,
every thought matters.

This sacred time informs my days,
nourishes my connection to divine beings
on this and other planes,
awakens my senses,
and keeps me humming
in tune with the universe.

THE VIEW FROM RAMAPRIYA'S WINDOW

She sits at the top of the hill
looking out at city, sea and sky.
Below
planes take off and land,
BART trains and buses,
trucks and cars
carry others about their busy business
while she
sitting with the birds
in the tops of the trees
lives a different pace
sips tea, eats fruits,
ruminates, meditates,
processes,
creates,
taking in
and giving out.
Being.

MORNING COMPOSITION

In my symphony today
the voices of friends
fresh strawberries
sunshine in a lovely patch on my desk
the sound of the ocean
new leaves on the rose bush
hot tea
embracing branches
sweet memories
and it's only just begun.
Oh, let this music play
and play and play.

Turning Pages

The flutist speaks of cycles in life as in music
then plays with his whole body,
gracefully dips to catch the low notes
onto his toes for the highs.
The pianist plays in her blue gown
her arced hands touching the keys,
now delicately, now forcefully.
He and she, a duet
their music weaving into one.
But my eye is caught by another
who sits slightly behind her,
attracted not so much by his good looks
as by the quality of his watching.
Dark eyes intent on the musical score,
he sits erect, completely still,
until on cue he rises and
holding his pale pink tie with his right hand
reaches over with the left to turn the page
forward or back, then,
left hand now on the tie
returns to his seat to watch
until the next time to rise.

I listen.
I have come to the mountain,
gazed at this snow covered Sanctuary,
source of power and comfort.
I drank the crystal water from the spring
source of the river, source of life.
I have whispered prayers,
walked through a cloud of skyblue butterflies
fluttering over swampy ground.

I have eaten food planned for five,
each meal a feast for the eyes as well as the palette,
wholesome food to nourish the body
lovingly prepared by one taking the role of Mother-God,
the Divine Feminine, Mary, Quan Yin,
as the dear one for whom it was intended lies
on her bed, wanting to be on this mountain
which has so long been calling.
A third friend keeps vigil at her side
giving comfort and support
and others hold the space
offering poems and prayers in this time of transition.
A sacred circle, sacred cycle.

We play our roles,
keep up the dance,
sometimes mother-goddess,
sometimes beloved-child, receiver of the gifts
sometimes artist-musician-player
sometimes page-turner, microphone-holder,
watcher, listener, poet,
transformer or transformed,
keeper of the space.

The flutist and pianist play on.
The page-turner in his pink tie sits, rises, sits.
The last movement, as promised,
reflects the beginning
until the last note sounds
and the audience sits in still rapt attention,
attending,
holding the space
in which such beauty continues to exist
even when the sound is gone.

RSVP

Hafiz, I received your invitation
and I want to come, but hesitate.
Wakened by the rosy glow of morning
I lift the blinds to view the green
of earth's winter renewal,
see the plump red hips—fruit of the rose bush,
enough goodness to give me a rush most days,
but this morning that rush is overwhelmed
by an ache in my heart.
What can I put on the table today
save that—a heavy heart,
a bowl of tears?

But then . . .
what else would one bring to a wake?
And so I come, Hafiz.
I come to join my friends,
to join with strangers.
Together we shall make a heady wine of the tears,
eat the nourishing fruit of the mature rose,
grateful for the wisdom,
grateful for the renewal,
grateful for the sharing
of heartaches as well as pleasures
and with our hearts open
it is sure to be
another great party.

Visiting the Sea with Miss Dickinson

Might I stand like you, dear Emily,
as the Tide rises over my shoes,
my waist, my shoulders?

Did the Sea move for you as it does for me,
in and out, washing sand
from beneath my feet,
leaving me slightly off balance?

Were you ever bowled over
by the crashing waves, tumbled
until you didn't know which way was up,
left torn and frightened on the sand?

Did you have to learn, as I did,
to dive beneath the turmoil
and rise on the other side,
there to be held, rocked, lifted,
accepting and accepted
by that expansive Vastness?

Do I, dear Emily, understand at all
the Pearls you offer in your poem?
Would you understand mine?

IN GRATITUDE TO THE GODDESSES OF SPIRIT

Oh, my friends,
my beloved Morning Friends,
what may I say you are to me?
You are the glowing, rosy light of dawn,
my morning tea,
awakening me to each new day.

You are my jesters, my jokesters,
lightening my load with laughter;
my monks and priestesses,
my spirit guides.

You are my wings,
my transportation to other realms,
opener of doors,
windows to new vistas.

You are my flute, my drums,
playing the songs, melodic, harmonious,
thrumming, drumming,
keeping the beat.

You are my gardeners and my garden,
nourishing my blooming and my fruiting.
You are my fruit, sweet and tangy,
setting my taste buds on fire.

You are my lions,
my guardians of the gate, my safety;
in your presence I am free
to be all I am.

You are my reflecting pool,
taking me into your depths
and revealing to me
my true self.

You are my beloved
And we are One.

A BLESSING ON THE SACRED SPACE

Under the trees we danced.
We danced for the departed.
We danced for troubled souls.
We danced for the children and the not yet born.
We danced for our own pleasure.
On the grass we danced barefoot and shod.
With sun and moon looking down we danced.
We danced for the earth.
With peace in our hearts we danced.
We danced for one another.
We danced for joy!
And when I lifted my arms to follow
the qi gong movements the energies of the air
vibrated against and through my skin
so palpable
so strong
I swear
I could hear it hum.

IGNITED

Some days I feel rather helpless
but not this day.
Perhaps it is the full moon
perhaps the connection
On the Call
fueling the internal flame
eternal flame
causing it to burn
and me to feel
strangely powerful
filled with a healing energy
that radiates
encompasses the planet
holding all the dear ones
my dear ones
your dear ones
and their dear ones
all precious beings
in healing wholing
fiery energy.
Sitting in silence
writing these words
feeds the flame
until it glows
white hot
pure
white light
for which
I
thank you.

KUNG FU GIRL

I am waiting for Kung Fu Girl
to tell her story
waiting for the paper cranes to fly
spinning plates
balanced on long poles
poetry and apps
photographs and audio files
spinning plates
Gramma's Walk
publication inspiration
Moon Song quilts
swirling cranes
Kung Fu Girl
spinning plates
can't let them fall
spinning plates
and waiting for the calm
waiting for the time to breathe
waiting for the words
of my next poem.
Beside me the candle flame
lights the serene face of Quan Yin
and I look to the sky
where rosy clouds drift slowly
calmly against the blue
and I am
breathing.

My Task

After the poetry reading
I try to choose one thing to write about
but the world is so lush and delicious—
the grasses so green,
the trees so majestic,
daisies hover in the green meadow,
pale pink lilies float on the pond,
blue columbine, magenta cranesbill,
orange calendula, purple petunias—
peach, pink, coral, scarlet,
blues, purples, yellows—
so many colors bursting out
in the garden beds,
all glowing in the moist light
under a white-gray sky
and all I can do—
the most important thing I can do
today and everyday—
is saturate myself in the wonder and glory
and add one more breath of joy
to this magnificent world.

HOW CAN I KEEP WRITING THE SAME POEMS?

I know it is May again.
I know this profusion of blooming
has happened countless times before.
I know that each time I look through the window
or walk into the garden
I will see the same vibrant display of blossoms
that has made my heart sing ten thousand times before
   —at least a hundred times just yesterday.
So how is it that each time takes me a little by surprise?
How is it that we can never say too many times,

   I love you?

Nature as Sacred

First November Rain

Rain softly falling on the roof
all through the night
a symphony of molecules, h²o
falling into the morning
onto the dry golden grasses
the copper redwood needles
colors glowing under gray skies
still spilling rain onto —
into the summer baked earth.
Molecules mixing with molecules
nutrients and water
taken up by the roots
quickening the hungry thirsty plants.
Molecules of saturation
satisfaction relief pouring out
into the fresh moist air
into my ears, my eyes, my heart
sending molecules of gratitude
and joy into the universe.

Strange Partners

After the rain
the sun's fire
is caught by droplets
on the tips of redwood needles.
Now, who would have thought
that two such unlikely partners,
fire and water,
would create
such a joyful dance?

AUTUMN ON THE COAST

In this place autumn is
the time when plants,
gone dormant in the summer drought,
awaken, soak in the welcome rain.

On this crisp day my fingers ache
to dig into the soil
make the earth ready
for new plantings
that their roots might
deepen through winter
to be ready for spring.

With the dust now washed
from the summer's debris
it is a good time for clearing and
I itch to drag dead limbs
from the forest floor
clearing pathways
and vision ways
between the stately trunks
beneath the branches
that the full vibrancy
of the woodland
may rise and shine.

LOVERS...

caught in a midnight embrace,
the moon and the redwood tree.

I Wanted to Write a Poem this Morning

I wanted to write a simple poem
about a simple kindness,
about seeing the beauty in what's there
and what's not there,
about what acceptance does
to the air in a room,
the air in the world,
how it makes it so much easier
to breathe
to be.

I wanted to write a poem this morning,
but I can't find the words except,
Did you see that golden color in the sky
just before the sun came sparkling
through those redwood branches?
Did you hear that first bird call?

Water

One droplet
on the tip
of a leaf
reflecting
containing
sustaining
the world.

Late September Morning

Rain sings me awake
whispering
sweet promises of green,
kissing, kissing, kissing
the summer parched earth,
softening the outer crusts of seeds,
soaking into cracks and crevasses
to caress the dormant roots,
which tingle at the touch,
shoot juicy signals
to waiting stems and leaves.
It's time…
It's time…
It's time…
Leaves, roots, seeds, rain, me…
all humming
in tender harmonic vibration.

Just Look

White clouds,
sun sparkling on
the redwood needles,
and daisies,
daisies, daisies.
Another great show
this morning
and all I have to do
is wake up.

GOOD DAY IN THE GARDEN

Something about pulling weeds
something satisfying
about grasping
that sweet spot at the top of the root
just below the surface of the moist soil
and pulling with a steady gentle force
until I feel that root, bit by bit,
release its hold on the earth
and come out whole in my fingers.

Not unlike the satisfaction
of finding that just right word for a poem,
or the *aha* when the muddle of information
I am trying to grasp
suddenly slips into place
and I understand. . .
something satisfying,
a wish fulfilled,
a small goal achieved.

Then there's the satisfaction
of the completed poem,
the concept understood,
or the garden clear of weeds,
chosen plants standing
with room to grow
in the rich black earth.

SECOND STORY VIEW

Whirling wall of redwood boughs
stirred by the wind
echoing the cosmic dance
of everything.

Why I Can't Garden in the Mornings

I have a book to complete,
tight deadline,
no time for gardening, but
before I begin the long day's work
I take my cup of tea to the deck
for a breath of morning air.
I can't resist a closer look
at the blush on a yellow rose,
so, still in my bedroom slippers,
I step out into the garden,
smell the rose,
pull a single weed,
    then another.

Next thing I know
it's noon and I have enough weeds
and prunings to fill a large wheelbarrow,
a sink full of chard,
berries to freeze,
a mental list of garden tasks
pleading urgently for attention.
My tea, still on the deck, is cold,
my slippers are grubby
and now I need a shower,
    but, oh!
What a morning I've had!

The Un-watched Plant

While my eye was on
the swelling delphinium spires
preparing for their grand display
the iris below the blackberries
quietly burst into bloom.

In Disguise

Again today
the sun is shrouded.
I sigh a lament
as I look into the garden.
Delphinium plants
grow large and lush,
blackberries shoot
branches like fireworks
in all directions,
new leaves put a blush
on the rose bush,
and the pear tree
is ablaze with blossoms.
Fog clears from my eyes as,
in all of these,
I see the fire
of the sun.

Gifted Again

Gray morning.
No visible sun.
Rain steady on the roof.
The trees stand guard,
tall, dark, mysterious.
At their edge
a patch of late daisies
reflects the sky
and my heart
gratefully accepts
the gift of another day.

May Day

The first of May
and all around the plants,
both wild and cultivated,
go mad in celebration,
bursting out in sprays
and blooms, colors
vibrant enough to shout,
or softly, gently, sing
their praise to spring.
Wild lilacs and iris,
cranes bill and coral bells,
daisies and roses,
callas and blackberries,
raspberries, delphiniums,
geraniums, blue-eyed grass,
and green, so much green,
everywhere, in every direction.
The sights so overwhelm me
that for a moment I simply
close my eyes and drink in
the sweetly fruity scent
of a single rose
and quietly hum
my own praise to spring.

Floating Lamps

On the pond
the water lilies bloom,
pale pink petals illuminated
by the glow of their own
golden centers.

AH, HAFIZ

You are so right.
The sun does not say
to the earth,
"You owe me."

But look!
Under that brightly lit sky
the earth sends up
sweet hyacinths,
a swath of daffodils,
calla lilies,
calendula.

Here it is,
barely spring,
and already
I see
a whole lot of kissing
going on.

JOY REFLECTED

The predawn sky
left its color on a cloud
of wild iris in the meadow.
You smile
and I radiate happiness.

STILLNESS

When
like now
there is no wind
not a branch swaying
nor leaf stirring
from the tops of the redwoods
to the iris blades
reflecting in the glassy surface
of the pond
not the tiniest movement
only stillness
it is as if
the earth is holding her breath
and I find myself
suspended in unison
waiting . . .

Slowly the sun
climbs up through the branches
growing brighter
bolder.
Now and then a bird
or pair of birds
dashes
from one tree to another
as if to get a better view
but the stillness holds
holds
holds
waiting
waiting . . .

being.

REFRESHMENT

Rain falling
through the night
soothing my sleep
washing away
the summer's dust,
gently soaking
the crusted earth,
absorbed by thirsty roots,
plumping the parched
leaves of laurels
and rhododendrons,
stimulating grasses
to send out new shoots,
seeds to swell and sprout,
racing up the cambium
layers of the redwoods
along the branches
into the needles
to kiss the sky.

RASPBERRIES

Gone only for a weekend,
two days and a half,
but the raspberries,
no more than bare red sticks
when I left,
are now full
with new green leaves.
What greater sign of love
than that?

Skunk Remains

On the woodland trail
we came upon the remains
of a skunk, a mound
of black and white fur
and exposed bones,
reeking strongly
but still less offensive
than the beer bottle,
soda can or plastic
potato chip bag.
The skunk will rot
absorbed into the earth
to feed new generations
of plants, then animals,
in balanced design.
Nature does not make trash.

The Poppy's Dance

Two days ago the poppy bloomed,
vibrant and fiery red.
Rains bowed it
nearly to the ground,
but today,
lifted by celestial music,
it turns back to face the sky.
I open my heart to hear.

A Subtler Shade of Fall

The blackberry bushes cling tightly to the last fruits
which manage to turn dark, if not sweet.
The strawberries and blueberries are done.
Even the fall raspberries are meager now,
the last pears, juicy and succulent,
ripened on the kitchen counter, now a memory,
and the other day I picked the last of the apples.

Most of the orchard leaves, turning subtly rosy, gold or brown
before they dropped, have passed along with summer fruits.
Sweet pea pods cling to the drying vine and seed heads
of weedy plants blow hither and yon to lodge in likely places.
With each breeze the redwoods, towering evergreen overhead,
shower us with crunchy needles, hitting the dry earth
where brown grasses lie dormant.

Here on California's coast, autumn does not come
in a blazing show, a fiery dance of celebration between
the lushness of summer and stark beauty of a snowy winter.
No, here it is a quiet winding down, a stretching out
of the long dry summer months, a subtle, subdued waiting.
Change is in the air all right, a sense of expectation,
as we savor the gifts of the season just past, and awaken
a longing for the rains of winter that will bring renewal.

Lit by the Sun

Tall grasses and daisies
stand upside down
in the still pond.

LOVE AFFAIR

I sat in the sacred classroom
my own passions stirred
by the words and processes
as through the window
I watched the wind whip
the golden seed heads
of the grasses
into a frenzied broth.
Then,
accidentally taking
the long way home,
I watched as mile after mile
the gentle wind caressed
the rolling grassy hillsides.
The wind my breath.
The earth my body.
Such sweet love making.

SEPTEMBER

the ground parched
from summer drought,
grasses dry and brown
        wait.
            …wait.

Standing tall in the morning mist
redwood trees collect
drops of moisture
which the breeze releases
onto my roof as I lie in bed
grateful for this promise
of winter rains to come.

SECOND-HAND RAIN

Rain all night,
steady, gentle.
I step into
the morning light,
the air cool, fresh.
On the redwood needles
drops of water hang,
glistening,
then fall,
some to the ground,
echoing the rain
in slow motion.
Others bounce
off lower water-laden
branches to spray
pinpoints of mist,
a thousand droplets
lit by the sun.

I would be
the drop that frees
thousands to shine.

GARDEN TRYST

So sweetly the moon
kissed the pale petunias
and left them blushing.

AFTER THE DROUGHT

~1
A bank of darkening clouds
blush pink along the top.
Through an opening the sun
focuses its last rays
a glowing white hot ember
on a slate blue hearth.

~2
Lone Calla lily lifts her face
to catch the drops
of precious rain.

~3
The sun goes down
in secret today
hidden by a curtain of rain.
Sleep sweetly all.

~4
Water spilling over stone.
Raindrops rippling the surface
of the newly filled pond.
The apple trees smile.

~5
Bright sun, blue sky, breeze,
ten times ten thousand rain drops
caught in the fingers of the towering trees
twinkle like fairy dust.

WEDDING PARTY

Surely she is a bride
that redwood
with her family gathered
in a circle around her.
See how gracefully the boughs hang
'round her slender trunk
and how the clematis,
blushing the softest pink,
cascades in sprays?
The perfect bridal bouquet.

SCORPION

Yesterday I held
a scorpion in my hand,
uncovered as I pulled apart
a rotting redwood log—
mulch for my blueberries.
I thought he was a grub
and picked him up,
glad I was wearing heavy gloves
although, folded up as he was,
he was not prepared to sting me
and in my hand he stayed that way,
folded into a neat little bundle
neither of us ready to do battle.
Freeing him I wondered
how many times we fight
just because that's what
we're prepared to do.

Soul Sisters

I am content
strong
stable
like the trunk of the redwood
swaying with graceful movement
as the wind stirs
its higher branches
echoing the restlessness
in my heart
eager to birth
the new possibilities.

First Signs

Just yesterday
I saw the first sign
of red coiled leaves
new leaves that will soon spread
into lily pads
floating on the water of the pond
red undersides
glossy green tops
all fresh and new with promise
of the blooms to follow
the glowing blooms
softly radiating
pink white golden light.
For now
the promise is enough.

NIGHT VISION

I get up in the night
and in the familiar darkness
ease my way up the stairs
to stand before
the cathedral window,
stand before
the sight of tall black trees
holding up a canopy of stars,
stand before this sight that
steals my breathe away
then blows it gently back
making me a part
of the great mystery.

SUN CIRCLE

The morning sun
warms my skin
as it warms and feeds
the leaves of the berry bushes
the grasses and weeds
which feed the deer
and rabbits.
It warms the black
feathers of the raven
and the robin
and the water of the pond
with the lilies and frogs
all of us One with the earth.
I am grateful.

Eternal Promise

A quick rain shower passes.
To the east the tips of the redwoods,
ignited by the sun's last rays,
glow golden against the dark clouds. . .

and then . . .
as if that were not splendor enough for one evening
the glow slides from the treetops
and in a heart beat
a luminous rainbow
arcs over the dark trees
arcs in full spectrum against the deepening sky
vibrant and glorious.

Transformation

Mottled sky
the earth and all its beings
softly grayed
when suddenly the sun
lights the white-pink blossoms of the tallest rose
bounces off the blackberry leaves
sets fire to the calendula
and everything comes into crisp
multi-layered definition.

Morning Show

Great clouds this morning,
floating, shifting,
performing their dance
against the backdrop
of flawless blue.
Clouds gray, buff
and rosy beige
haloed with glowing pearl.
Who shall I thank
for the show?

Big Enough

It's just a small pond,
as ponds go,
good for minnows
and salamanders,
quite popular with frogs,
dragonflies,
and small children.

Just a small pond
in the redwoods,
big enough for lily pads
and tall yellow iris.

Just the right size
to sit beside and ponder
to wonder at how
such a small pond
can hold those redwoods
and that sky.

Wow!

Did you see
the perfect peach glow
where the sun kissed the sea
goodnight?

How could I not
love this life?

Amazing!

Day after day
the sun and clouds
play that same venue
at the sea's horizon—
a perpetual engagement.

Layers

Yesterday the wind
whipped the trees to a frenzy.
Today they stand eerily still
as white clouds race overhead
and I, looking through my window,
sit outwardly calm
with so many thoughts
tumbling
in my head.

As One

In the cold this morning
fire and water dance together,
leap in sparkling droplets
off the roof of the barn,
leave glittering tracks
across the frosting
of snow on the deck,
and on my window pane,
one lone drop of condensation
brings the enchanting show
up close.

What I Choose to Notice

The morning light
on the drying eggshells
in the kitchen window
catches my eye
and takes my breathe away.
Who would have thought
such a simple thing
could bring such
pleasure?

ECHO

Echoing the circle of the sun
pale cream petals, rays of light,
the golden glowing center,
dancing fluted edge,
like flames off the sun disc,
the daffodil
salutes the sun.
I do believe a fanfare
rings from the jaunty
stamen and sepals.

Halleluiah!

Halleluiah!

Halleluiah!

TANGLED

In the night the moon,
large and bright,
appears to be entangled
in the branches of the redwoods.
I lie wakeful,
my mind entangled
in lists of things to do,
but breathing slowly,
deeply, into my heart
I know it is all illusion—
heart, mind, moon
all free.

The Ancient Ones

I stand within the circle
of burned out stumps
of ancient redwoods
the majestic trees
long gone
to the sawmill
at the mouth
of the Gualala river
a sawmill itself
long gone as well
each tree now a circle
of second growth
the echo of the energy
of the ancient ones shimmers
a display for me
of what was.
Be careful
they say,
be careful.

Song for Today

Today the rain writes
lovely lines
pattering
its rhythmic song.
The earth,
and my heart,
drink gratefully.

ALIVE!

In high
creative mode
ideas electrically ignite
bouncing within me
until
every nerve ending
is awake,
alive,
tingling with excitement.

In such a state
I look up
and see myself
reflected in the redwoods
a moving wall of green.
Graceful branches bounce,
slender twigs twist
and
countless needles
shimmer
in the light.

Exploring
the
Mystery

SHARING

Walking along a road,
trees towering on either side
the light dusky with a tinge of rose,
suddenly to my right
a great white crane
swoops from a branch and glides
through the trees.
So brief is the vision
that it is almost unreal and yet it is
the most real and lasting moment
of the entire walk.
I write these words in a vain attempt
to share the moment.
We write words, take photos,
hoping to hold, to share,
but these images are no more than code;
dots and dashes, ones and zeros, colored pixels.
What we really want to share—
what we really want to hold,
is in the gap between—
is the no thing that is everything
which now and then slips through my mind
like the crane—
the only real thing.

IN THE ZONE

I wonder how the Great Creator
　　thought of clouds?
　　…made them able to hold water,
　　let it fall as rain or snow, sleet or hail?
　　…made them light enough
　　to catch the wind,
　　play chase across the sky,
　　or swing-the-statue, inventing new shapes,
　　…or pile in great heaps to roar with thunder,
　　…or stretch into delicate wisps, hardly there at all.
Was it in the plan for them
　　to play hide-and-seek with the sun,
　　and the moon and stars?
　　…or, maybe the best game of all,
　　to catch the light, dress up in all those colors:
　　grays and blues, roses and golds,
　　lavenders and even, at times, a hint of green,
　　glowing as if that light is their own doing.
I'll bet the Creator didn't think of it at all.
I'll bet it was just one of those
　　things that happens
　　when an artist is in the zone.

CLEANSING THE WORD

God.
Such a tricky word
with so much history.
This personalized stuff,
God as father,
loving or vengeful,
not benign,
the aged male,
white-bearded,
sitting on a throne
above us all,
decree-er of laws,
ruler over His Creation
is not for me.
And yet I cannot find
another word
that conveys
the immensity
of the absolute
Love and Light
that is
in its pure essence
　well…
　　　GOD.

LITTLE THINGS

So easy
to be brought down
by petty things
to a sense of angst,
of not enough,

but just as easily
it is the small thing—
the hovering dragonfly,
the laughter of my grandson,
the sweet taste
of the autumn raspberry—
that brings me
right back
to the edge
of the infinite.

AMAZING

how little it takes
to be in touch with the Divine.
Just open the door.

A Continuance

I am a continuance
of the grandmothers I never met
and the granddaughters yet to come
a continuance of sisters
blood sisters soul sisters
sisters on the call
in me air fuels the fire
water is the main ingredient of my body
water and earthly elements
calcium, phosphorous, amino acids
tiny molecules of bone, muscle, organs
but each of these is
in turn mostly empty space
a continuance of sky
and earth fire and rain
my body an illusion I am
a continuance of thoughts feelings ideas
poems spewed into the ether
caught by the energy that is me
run through in and out
weaving sparking joining
the continuance of the great dance
of all that is was and will be
the dance of yes!

ANY MODE

A mantra
a prayer
a silence
emptiness
a walk
a song
a dance
a ritual ceremony
what does the mode
of transportation matter
when it all takes you
to the same place—
that connection
deep within the heart
to what is most real
most alive
most important.

I DREAM

I dream that which dreams me.
I breathe that which breathes me.
I see that which sees me.
I am the knowing and the known.
I am the seed and the earth,
the fetus and the mother,
that which gives birth,
and that which is birthed.

Three times I carried within me
beings that were me and not me.
As her sisters before her,
the last emerged from my womb,
whole, complete, separate.
But as her small body relaxed onto mine
our breathing merged
and suddenly I sensed
her tiny limbs as my own.
I was her. I was me.
She was herself. She was me.
For that brief moment in time
I, in my physical body,
touched the infinite,
I within the cosmos within me.

Decades later I wonder,
what now lies within me,
unseen, unsensed?
What cosmic seeds
wait for expression?
What buds await my attention
to open into full glorious bloom?
What bridges?
What rainbows?
What poems?
What new-old myths want to be told,
to be given form?

Let me reach deep
into the stillness,
into the all-time no-time,
let me go deep into the invisible realms
and there be impregnated
that I may once again
birth cosmic wonders.

MEDITATION

Sitting in silence
the words weave through me
strands of colored ribbon
elements of earth, air, water, fire
the light of ancient stars
a newly emerging shoot pushing through life-giving soil
memories of your great-great-great-grandmother
dreams for my grandchild's grandchild's grandchild
their hands clasped through time
as they dance, encircling our circle
connections, sacred and forever
words, thoughts, prayers, silence
weaving them, and us, into a tapestry
of eternal being.

LOOKING FOR THE DOOR

I take my pen in my left non-dominant hand
and begin to write
    avoiding the paths worn smooth
    by what I know I know,
seeking the elusive depths of my essential self,
    less control,
    more presence,
slowed down
    to pay attention to the formation of each letter.
I might practice and become more facile with this hand,
    might even bring it to the point of those
    perfectly formed letters and words of my school years,
    but what would be the point?
One more grooved pathway of knowing
    what I already know,
    smooth and familiar.
Already this grows easier, more readable
    and the mystery beckons.

Step again, dear. Step further, deeper.
Step where there are no pens, no paper, no words.
Step deep into the paintings on the walls of the caves.

    Let go.

        Let go.

            The mystery will always be . . .

                    just that.

Pondering Form and Shadow

I look up and see,
above the hills in the day-lit sky,
right through the moon,
a wispy cloud-like vision without substance,
infinitesimal particles of spinning energy
holding the spherical space that is revealed
only by reflected light.
Like the child playing hide-and-seek
I close my eyes and disappear,
my body miniscule whirling particles,
pure energy holding this space
like the invisible moon in the vast blue,
I too am formless, no substance, no shadow.
In a moment of lucidity I am the moon,
the vastness . . . all that is.
In my most conscious moments
I am the light and there are no shadows.

After Reading an Article in EnlightenNext

Yes!

My brain strains
to understand the tales
of microtubules vibrating
in the space time continuum
consciousness before consciousness
ancient myths
Platonic virtues
shamanic dream states
Jesus and Buddha
quantum partners
meetings where the veil is thin
but
every now and then
the mists clear
and to my challenged western mind
just for an instant
it all makes perfect sense.

THE GOAL

is to hold the space
to be in the elusive gap
between thoughts
between heartbeats
the breath in the breath.
To try too hard
is to walk a tight rope
tense and uneasy
breathless
struggling for balance.
The way
is to relax with intention
into the stillness
to breathe and allow
to accept
to be.

A PRAYER

Speak to me this morning, cranes.
Too much history,
too many current events,
the expressionless sky,
a blank white space above the trees,
reflects the numbness in my mind.
This is one of those days when
filled with regret and shame
I want to retire from the human race.

Speak to me, cranes.
Call my spirit upward.
Give me wings to soar on the winds
that I may be renewed
to descend again
and along with you
make the ancient stories new.

PEACE ABIDES

The poet says peace
is there beneath the grass.
The thought pleases me, rings true,
sings through my body.
And if peace is beneath the grass, I think,
then it must also be beneath the rocks,
the desert sands, the forests,
the lakes, rivers, and great seas.
Peace must be the core,
the very stuff of earth,
the Heart.

The mystic says we are, each of us,
a puzzle piece of the planet;
we are our Mother Earth.
We are, each of us,
an expression of the earth,
an expression of peace
—or not.

In words we say,
Peace abides in me.
We hold a vision
a vision to manifest in action,
in the words we speak,
in the energy we use,
the purchases we make,
the food we grow and share,
the hands we extend,
the wounds we tend,
the joy we spread.

Peace abides in me.
Peace abides in the earth.
May I, as a piece of the beloved Mother,
manifest that truth,
may I be an unwavering expression
of Her true Heart.

YEARNING

Yearning… longing …
a wishing with one's whole heart …
… a striving to attain.

The scientists who test such things
tell us that the pleasure centers
in the brain shine their brightest
just before the catch,
just before the solution,
in that moment of high anticipation.

Can it be that we don't so much
want to be there as to be seeking?
Can it be that our best moments are those just before
reading the last page of a great book, just before
placing the last piece in a difficult puzzle, just before
removing the wrapping from a gift,
when what one is about to find is still unknown,
a thing of wonder which might be anything?

Or those precious moments of beginning,
holding the newborn in one's arms,
taking on a new job,
writing a new story or starting a quilt,
planting the seeds in the fertile earth,
when the possibilities, so full of promise,
are opened wide?

Those great *now* moments of being
so completely and utterly *in* the mystery.
Can it be that it is the yearning, the longing,
the mystery itself,
that which we almost,
but don't quite, know
that keeps us so sweetly,
so deliciously, alive?

THE DANCER RELEASED

Last night in my dreams
I was with one
who opened my eyes
untied my feet
introduced me to
the dancer hidden
so deeply within.

Last night in my dreams
I was with one
who is forever with me
for once you know
about the dancing
you can never again
not know.

BALANCING

On the edge of sleep
listening to the rain

hovering
in that mind-space
where nothing is
everything.

NEGATIVE

My friend speaks of finding joy
in the small crevices and cracks
of this angry place.
How often we see it that way,
the ugliness huge and overwhelming,
stifling and clouding our vision,
but in those moments when we are
walking among the redwoods,
gathering together in song,
standing on the dunes of the desert,
watching a child discover the pleasure of sand,
breathing in the beauty of the red rock canyons,
hearing the laughter of children at play,
mesmerized by the waves caressing the shore,
or more simply
when our eyes meet and our hearts open,
suddenly the vision shifts and we see.
We see that we have been looking
at the photographic negative;
the ugliness and anger are merely crevices
in an incredibly bountiful
and breathtakingly beautiful
world.

To Do the Work

To let the ego go,
to be even for one moment
free from the judgments
of society, prescriptions
and expectations
one puts upon oneself,
free from the awareness
even of body, of mind
so quiet, so still,
still enough to become
the rose, the tree,
the other,
then one might
know Heaven
might be able
to do the real work
of God.

SCIENCE OF SPIRIT

Not mind over matter,
not mind from matter,
but mind *and* matter
born simultaneously
in the first instance of consciousness,
a quantum collapse
in the split second after the Bang,
precursors of matter with innate properties
of spin, mass and charge,
precursors of mind with innate properties of
goodness, truth and beauty?
Some say it could be.
My mind says, Yes, it's true and I,
as in I, Consciousness, not I, Anna,
am a fractal of that first instance of consciousness,
a fractal containing the whole,
containing time before man
before life
before matter
when all was one,
containing instances of consciousness
of all that ever was and is
perhaps even all that will ever be,
which would explain how sometimes
I know what I don't know,
explain how I, Anna,
in moments of stillness
in moments of great emotion
can be so sublimely conscious
of the One that I AM.

Knowing

Mythologies, great wisdom traditions,
quantum physics, neurobiology,
conscious evolution, biosphere,
paradigm shift, epigenetics.
I read, I listen, I think, I feel —
the ideas, information, questions,
whirl and tumble inside my brain,
swell my heart,
expanding and exploding.
So big, so vast, so all encompassing,
but…
all I really need to do is
sit quietly with this one small flower,
    this newly opened rose,
and know that it
            is everything.

Emergence

In the silent pause between
the out breathe and the in breathe,
the moment between sleep and wakefulness,
between the first pecking inside the shell
and the emergence of the hatchling,
between before and after,
is the sweet magical instant
when everything
is absolutely possible.

MISSED

Through my window I saw
the first swell of the rose bud,
then saw it nearly ready,
even saw, from the back,
that the opening had begun,
all the time thinking,
the moment would come
when I would go out,
breathe in,
and fully enjoy the bloom,
but I was busy
reading about God.
Now I see the petals
are all gone.
How many opportunities
do I miss
to be fully present,
to enjoy,
to be kind?

DOG DREAMS

My dog talks in his sleep,
sometimes short yips,
last night a mournful eerie howl.

I wonder what he dreams,
what he thinks
in his walnut-sized brain—
a brain just big enough to know
the really important stuff.

I wonder if —
on those long afternoons,
when I think he's sleeping in the sun —
instead, he's listening to poetry
carried by the wind
or in the ravens' calls.

I wonder if all the animals —
perhaps even the trees —
have their own poetry societies
in which they share secrets
so profoundly simple that we
with our too big, too busy brains
can't begin to understand.

REGARDING STORY

We westerners,
so haughtily convinced
the world was nothing but matter,
materialism to the core,
now come to find that matter
is itself nothing, or nearly nothing.
Nothing is everything
and everything no-thing.
So we begin to re-story with
new names; particle, quark, matrix.
New stories of our ultimate
connectedness, once known
as Spirit, as God, as Holiness.
In our expanding shrinking world
we call in stories of other cultures
stories with other words,
all of us telling our stories,
stories of the same truth,
a truth the earth
has known all along,
that we are all One.

WHERE DO THE ANGELS DANCE?

How many angels can dance
on the head of a pin?
As many as choose to I should think, but
having tried it once,
would an angel choose to do it again,
especially given the variety
of dance floors that abound?

I believe angels often dance
on the tops of my redwood trees,
sometimes by the dozens,
leaping from swaying top to top
in a giggling game of tag,
or sometimes one lone angel
fills the whole sky
her misty robes floating between the branches.

I believe angels dance on the poppies and the roses,
holding hands and hopping lightly from petal to petal
voices chiming as they circle,
"Ring-around-the-rosie."

I believe angels dance
in the hands of the weaver, and the potter,
the woodworker, and the painter,
the farmer, and the baker,
in the heart of the compassionate,
the mind of the poet,
the dreams of the children.

I believe angels dance
any place they want to
any time they are invited.

IT'S A ROCKY WORLD

The poets dared my child-self out today,
Robinson Jeffers and the morning crew,
with poems and talk of rocks,
dared my child-self out to play
that three-to-six-year-old
for whom there are no veils,
who dwells in what adults call
the twilight world,
a world without a line between real and unreal.

In this twilight world
which most adults rarely glimpse
Jeffers saw the living rock
its passion, nobility, loveliness,
its past and future,
its separate almost eternal fate,
saw his own and his offspring's fate
so fleeting in comparison.

We humans egocentric as we are
have concocted story after story
of how this precious rock-based earth
was created especially for us,
as our home, our paradise, our school.

But my child mind asks,
What if it's the other way around
and it's all about the rocks?
What if the stones, once formed in that big bang
and cooled into their solid form,
got bored sitting for all those millennia
and began to manifest
life—fungi and lichens to paint their surfaces,
plants with roots to dig into them
and scratch the itchy spots,
to break them up a bit, change their forms?

What if rocks in a frenzy of manifestation
created human beings for nothing more
than their own entertainment
and then began to put into the minds
of these odd little beings—us, our minds—
crazy thoughts about moving some of them—the stones—
moving massive stones long distances,
and putting them in circles or pyramids,
towers or cathedrals or roads?
Put into the minds of these humans
thoughts of carving, polishing, trading,
deeming some precious, some plain?

What if we are nothing more
than a source of entertainment for the noble, eternal stones?
My child-self, the wise one
who keeps rocks on the window sill,
and in a bowl on the bookshelf, and a jar on her desk,
and in the garden, and around the pond,
and slips one into her pocket now and then
and kissed the stones of Beltony Circle
laughs at the recognition of a truth.
I speak the thought aloud to those who love
to tread with me in this twilight space
and without hesitation the child-self poets answer
Ah, then what we should do is dance all the more
so we don't bore the rocks.

THROUGH THE VEIL

I woke up
knowing
for a microsecond
the secret of everything
but as soon as the elation
became a thought
the unconsciousness of
wakefulness
swept it away.
Still
somewhere deep
I know I know
and these words float
in a wispy whisper
Live life
every second
as a prayer.

SHALL WE TALK?

I tap the keys.
Words—
surprising words—
float into the air
…from me?
…to me?
…through me?
Does not matter which
matters only that
as we dance
the universe and I engage
in this intriguing conversation.

Awesome Thought

Just before sunset I watch
the great gray clouds
blowing over the ocean,
the distant rain streaking down
cross-wise to the slanting rays
of the late afternoon sun,
and am in awe of the drama,
of the greatness of the cloud,
the vastness of sky, sea, and shoreline.

Suppose I did not know
the scientific explanations,
did not know about evaporation,
condensation, warm fronts,
cold fronts, had never seen
a weather map. Would I
feel closer to the gods?

Suppose I did not know
of planets, solar systems,
galaxies, orbits, the infinity
of the universe,
did not know of atoms, particles, quarks,
the astounding connection
of the minute with the vast.

Suppose I did not know
that science, after taking us
through all the explanations,
had come back to
the ultimately unexplainable,
to the most awesome thought of all,
that we ourselves are god,
that, indeed, there is
nothing that is not God.

Seeking Purpose

In My Prime

The wild rose,
its display of blushing
blossoms long past,
puts on a second show
nearly as spectacular,
red hips glowing,
swollen with nutrition.
Like the rose
my blush is gone
but not my beauty;
I too shine
with the allure
of a later season;
swollen with the wisdom
of experience.
I'll serve
a nourishing tea
for those who care to sip.

Turn Around

Born in the forties, growing up
in the shadow of the nuclear bomb,
rampant consumerism
wreaking its havoc on the environment,
a sixties flower child,
I fully expected that mine
would be the generation to end war,
to end hunger, to stop the ravaging
of our mother earth.

Now perilously close
to the conventional age of retirement,
I've never lost the dream of what can be
but somewhere along the way
I lost the expectation.
I began this year with an aching heart
a need to be more, do more, not give up.

As the year turns,
at this momentous solstice
marked by a lunar eclipse,
sun and moon and earth,
galaxy and solar system
at a magic moment in the dance,
I feel an excitement,
a reawakening of the expectation
that the dream can be fulfilled,
that humanity is on the brink
of something truly wonderful
and that instead of being about to retire
I am just beginning my true work.

Yellow Messages

Before the reading this morning
I walk into my garden
and cut a yellow rose
wet with the nighttime rains.
Placing it near my figure of Quan Yin
I notice through the window
three yellow iris standing guard
over the pond and then I open the booklet
and read, "Song to the Maize."

My mind goes to the yellow forehead of the mask
created as the vision of my-own-true-self.
I was not happy with that yellow,
not accepting of my creative vision,
but here I am faced with yellow times three,
lovely yellows. Oh silly me.
I am judging again, self-consciously doubting.

When, in ceremony, I took off
the mask of my-own-true-wise-self
and asked of it, "Oh wise one,
what is it I need to know?"
The answer came,
"You know all you need to know.
You have always known. Trust that."

And still I question, Can that be true?
Am I trying too hard to find
some huge and difficult path,
some task to do, role to play
in this great change
when my own truth is to keep walking,
keep creating, keep sharing,
keep loving, in my own quiet way?

I grow more and more in tune
to that voice within, the one
that has brought me to this point
where I now stand with a clear
and loving heart, ready for the work.

Now I remember, too, a vision
of liquid pouring from my ears,
a cleansing, a clearing.
Okay, I get it. I get it,
Oh Wise One. I am listening.

IF I AM SINCERE

Oh, how important I am
one little leaf in a forest of trees
a small grain of sand on miles of shore
a tiny drop of water in a vast sea
a miniscule particle among billions of particles
so minimal
I am almost nothing
and yet,
if I am sincere
if I am true to my own nature
as leaf, as sand, as drop, as particle,
as human heart,
then I am everything
and all will be well.

SECONDARY WORKS OF ART

In my mind I paint the water lily,
the delicate change of color
from palest lavender-pink
to glowing white,
paint the lily pad, green
tinged with maroon,
paint the reflection in the still pond.
But never do the brush strokes
on paper equal that image
in my mind, nor does the image
in my mind compare
to that in the natural world,
the work of a true master.
And yet I believe my seeing,
my imaging, my painting
must be important
else why would I be so
driven to keep trying?

TRAPPED BY BIOLOGY

In a holographic world
my electro magnetic heart
connects with the electromagnetic fields
of other hearts,
of trees and roses and salamanders
of the earth, the sun, the solar system
sending and receiving,
but at any sign of danger,
real or imagined,
my brain automatically shifts to defense mode
triggering my heart to do the same,
shutting down my ability to reason,
defensiveness cloaked in common sense,
revenge as justice,
old patterns supported by
ancient field energies,
supported by my culture's herd mentality,
trapped by the automatic reflexes
of my own biology.
No wonder I cry to God for help
to break free
back to what,
somewhere deep
I know is possible,
the positive,
the loving coherent signals
that are also available
to my connected heart.

MY PATCHWORK LIFE

Spreading my life
like a patchwork quilt
I can point out the dark pieces,
the night my Daddy left,
my oldest daughter's teenage angst,
my own,
the troubled spot in the marriage
when we wondered
if we'd make it through,
the unexpected death of a dear friend.

But I can also point to the bright spots,
the births of all the babies,
daughters, then grandchildren,
precious moments of their growing,
the light in Emmett's eyes looking up
at the redwood trees,
Violet singing in the orchard,
Jacob leading the parade with pampas grass,
the family gathering in celebration,
quiet moments laughing with the man
I've loved thirty-five years and counting,
the rich color and texture of that lasting love,
a centerpiece,
moments of ecstasy when my heart
has opened to the universe
or the intimate.

Each memory an intricate part of the whole,
the darks rich in their own way
making the lights glow brighter,
the transitional pieces of everyday life
holding it all together
in a wondrous masterpiece
of joy.

My Grandchildren

She calls herself Poet-Girl
this round cheeked child
who leaves me messages
about the wind.
I call her Best Beloved.

He calls himself M1-the-Awesome,
tow-headed creator
of the myth
of the spider planet.
I call him Light of My Life.

He calls himself Funky-Noodle,
a lanky young man,
once curly-haired cherub,
who sang before he talked.
I call him my Great Joy.

They call me Moma,
these children of my children.
I share what I know,
give them pens, paints,
fabrics, thread,
stand back and watch
the creative explosions.

They call themselves
a new name everyday,
changing, growing,
delighting, astounding,
bursting my heart.
I call them Sacred.

ANTIDOTE

Poised on the edge
of what is to be;
personally,
new business,
new grandchild,
circles expanding.
Nationally,
people speaking out,
standing up for justice,
numbers growing.
Can we shift?
Universally,
an awakening,
spreading awareness
of our true nature
as beings of light.

I teeter on the brink,
unsettled,
adrenaline buzzing,
mind antsy.
What to do
in this space?
This almost but not quite
time?
Breathe.
Visualize the good.
Take in the color of the morning sky,
the sun on the tops of the redwood trees,
slice the apples for the winter's pies,
and don't forget
to enjoy the sweet taste
of summer's last peach.

Yesterday...

was one of *those* days.
The irritations piled up;
    not sure I like the new haircut,
    the software ate the latest version of my project,
    the dog snarled at another on the trail,
    the burrito place was closed
        so I had to cook when I didn't plan to,
    the recycling center has moved...
        eight miles out of town.
All petty stuff
    except maybe for that recycling center thing,
    but still I'm agitated,
    hard to remember
    to hold the vision of the sun on the leaf,
    the glow of the rose blossom.
Before I sleep
    I remember who I am,
    remember the Divine Light
    and send blessings
    to those who need healing,
    to those I love,
    to all beings.
My sleep is deep and sound
    and in my dreams
    bouquets are delivered to my door.

GOD'S OVEN

It was not punishment.
I knew that.
God would not be like my capricious father,
finding something funny one minute,
and raging in anger the next,
punishing for things over which
I had no control.
God was Love
and so this pain was not
to strike me down,
but make me strong,
make me something more,
something needed in the world.
Still it puzzles me —
how is it that some
placed in God's oven
come out hard,
brittle as unleavened bread,
and others soft and tender
as the lightest soufflé ?

FEEDING DREAMS

The magic happens
the poet said,
when you feed your dream fire.

Feed your dreamfire?
Or feed your dream fire?
What do dreams eat?
Toasted marshmallows
and melted chocolate?
Sweet yummy s'mores?
Or raw gristly meat?
Something of substance
chewy and challenging?

Or moonlight
and starlight?
The fire of lightning
as it streaks through the sky?
Ingredients of magic;
illumination, imagination,
charm, power?

Feed your dream.
Feed your dream fire.
Feed it with passion.
Keep your dreamfire glowing
on the hearth
of your heart.

BUSY WEEK

Leaving soon
lots to do
pick the pears
feed the worms
wash the sheets
answer the emails
pack the clothes
go to the dentist
write the talks
keep the passion
make the slides
finish the project
back-up the files
check the schedule
confirm the plans
pick the peas
breathe it in
and the berries
let it out
stay in touch
stay in touch
none of it matters
without love
none of it matters
without joy
it's where I am
what I've chosen
breathe it in
let it out
in the moment
stay with love
stay with love

Night Pleasures

I welcome the night,
the silence,
the stillness,
the sweet sleep that comes easily,
even the two AM trek
to the bathroom
with a stop at the kitchen sink
for a short sip of water
as I glimpse the night sky.
In fact, I've come to look forward
to that interruption in my slumber
for on a clear night
the view of the tree tips
kissing the stars
is breathtaking
and I drift back to bed
and sleep
embraced by the universe.

HAVING IT BURN BOTH WAYS

Raven, bring your flint.
This box has got to go.
Over the years I've cut windows,
added doors,
thought I'd shredded these old walls,
but still I find myself inside,
limited by old messages.
Cackle, Raven.

Cackle at the ridiculousness
of thoughts taken at face value.
Just because the child was happiest
in the house with the privy in the back yard
does not mean I should not love my plumbing.
Just because wealth came with loss,
just because old narratives
said only selfish greedy girls wanted more,
that having more meant someone else had less,
does not mean any of it is true.

The dream is created as we go along.
A vision of plenty creates plenty.
Joy begets joy.
Cackle, Raven, and strike your flint.
Burn this box.
Make the fire hot, hot, hot!
Burn away the walls,
purify the core of my being
and let me rise from the ashes,
ready for abundance.

Then strike again, oh Raven.
Strike again
and set my dreams on fire!

VESSEL

What am I inside this body?
Not the me I see in the mirror certainly,
nor even the me in my mind,
a little firmer, more youthful than the mirror me.

Am I the me I see in the eyes
of my grandchildren, capable of miracles,
the Moma who can mend anything,
concoct a Swedish dress on short notice,
or babble baby language?

Am I the me in my mother's eyes,
a little child grown into aging woman,
accomplished and dependable?

Or the me in my lover's eyes,
life partner, years of passion easing into comfort
and a quieter sort of ever-present joy?

Am I the me in my daughters' eyes,
role of protector-guide long given up,
but still an ember to flame when summoned?

Or the me in the eyes of friends, new and old,
with whom I share the joys of both
memory and discovery,
of wisdom growing with the years?

I am all of that, yes,
but like the water is not the ocean,
or the river, or the raindrops
I am also not that.
I am bigger, brighter,
more than all my roles
for even without these precious reflections,
connections, experiences,

I am.

Violet Time

Like Walt Whitman listening
to the learned astronomer
I read the books
about mindfulness, love,
being in the now,
the power of the heart,
my study interrupted
by a thumping down the stairs,
six-year-old Violet Grace
already smiling
ready for the day.

She sings as she eats
as she draws
as she creates gifts
for her daddy
for the new neighbors
for me.
She won't be rushed
engaged in whatever she does
with her whole being
her whole heart.

As Whitman turned from
the auditorium to the sky
I leave my books
and listen to Violet singing
as she sits alone in the orchard
heart wide open
being . . .
everything I hope to be.

WATCHING A DRAGONFLY WITH EMMETT

He sits on my lap.
Just over a year,
his words are few.
"Airplane" he says.
and then, as the winged creature
comes closer, "Anty."
It zooms away, "Airplane."
Returns to hover, "Anty."
"Airplane."
"Anty."
"Anty."
"Airplane."
"Airplane-anty."

Two years later
his first ride
in a real airplane,
we look down upon the clouds.
"It can't rain on us," he says,
his innocent wonder
my portal to wisdom.

FINDING THE CALM
(or Thanksgiving with a Three-Week-Old Granddaughter)

My mind!
My time!
I've been fast tracking,
by-passing the quiet cushion, skipping yoga.
Today I say, "I will go slow."
The busy grandchildren have gone home.

No one to tend now, I light a candle,
study the graceful folds in Quan Yin's gown
and sit breathing in and out.
But my mind still scurries here and there,
over the wonders, the snags,
re-tastes the joys of these past days,
burrows into the anxieties,
lists of things to do in the days to come.
So much, such big dreams.
Can we? Will we?
And my friends with troubles,
what can I say to them?
Breathe in. Breathe out.

Finally my mind lights
not empty but caught in a moment,
when after being head cook,
sitting with my family around the Thanksgiving table,
I claim privileges and take the squirming baby.
Eating my dinner one handed I rock and sooth her,
watch her settle into sleep across my lap.
As we eat and converse and laugh
I look down upon her tiny form,
the sweet profile of her baby face,
so relaxed,
so serene,
so peaceful,
so perfect.
Just remembering
I find myself in total bliss.

WHAT IS MY NAME?

My name is infant.
My name is grandmother.
My name is old soul.
My name is evolving.
My name is poet.
My name is she who has no words.
My name is grace.
My name is shame.
My name is lover of trees.
My name is driver on the blacktopped roads.
My name is holder of the sacred spaces.
My name is creator.
My name is destroyer.
My name is regret.
My name is celebration.
My name is complexity.
My name is simplicity.
My name is all that is.
My name is not.
I am not my name.
I am.

Thoughts on Permanent and Impermanence

A mere thirty years ago
there was no Internet,
no laptop computers, no cell phones,
no DNA testing to tell us
who is genetically connected to whom.

The records carved in stone
are no more than semi-permanent.
We live in a morphing world,
like a flip-book in which the images
continually change,
images flashed on a screen—
one thousand years of art in sixty seconds.

We, and all our creations,
are but another flash.
And yet the words of ancient poets
soothe our souls,
the paintings on the walls of caves
speak to us, connect us,
not unlike our daily communication
made possible by Internet,
cell phones and fiber optics.

It does not matter today
whether I tend the garden,
create computer graphics, knit socks,
write poetry, or play the harmonica.
It matters that I am,
Here, being, connecting with you,
with past and future,
part of this always Now
and always changing Oneness
that is everything.

It matters that
in my flashing impermanent moment
I love with my heart overflowing.

PLAYING WITH FIRE

It's a dangerous game
filled with risks
but what alternative other than
sitting out the dance
sitting immobile in the shadows.
A most dangerous game
that will certainly leave you
changed
singed perhaps
or worse
possibly even consumed with its enticing flames
but how else can one hope to illuminate the shadows
how else is one tested, strengthened, enlightened
how else can one hope to be fully alive
how else can one create a life worth living
if one does not make that dangerous choice
to dance with the fire?

PEACE CRANES

Life
    squares of newspaper
    bad news good news
Fold and press
    shopping lists
    eggs broccoli lettuce milk
Turn and fold
    store receipts
    working notes
    pages from a catalog
    things I need
    things I don't
Crease, open, fold again
    to-do lists
    knitting instructions
    packing slips
    endearing notes
It matters not what
    meat potatoes
    sorrows joys
    flotsam jetsam
    fears regrets
Fold it in
    bits of life
    the humdrum
    the bizarre
    the disturbing
    the enlightening
    all of life
Fold in and over
    everyday
    every day
Fold it in

Folding and holding
    remembering
    imagining
    transforming
Fold and open
    this visible form of my intention
    to keep peace in my heart
    in our world
Make peace with my hands
    One thousand cranes
    One thousand days
Forever

EMBERS

Embers of yesterday's fires,
flames of exciting plans
and projects
stoked with joyful anticipation
through the busy day
then left
not quite finished,
burned through my restless sleep.

Toward morning I left them
safely banked
to drift into
a deeper sleep from which I
waken refreshed
with the breath to blow
those still glowing sparks
into today's productive flames.

October 13, 2014

On or about this day
sixty-nine years ago
I chose to be born
on this earth in human form.
I chose to be female,
to love and be loved,
to climb and to stumble,
to learn and to grow,
to give birth and to nurture,
to create and evolve.

Today I choose again
I choose to open my eyes
to the coral rose outside my window
its singing color, sweet scent,
the rose itself choosing to bloom again
this late in the year.
I choose its backdrop of deep green redwood trees
and blue sky studded with glowing clouds,
pulled by the wind into white cotton strands as I watch.

I choose to rise like the sun another day
to hold this human form
breathe the air
drink the waters
walk the earth
embody the divine fire
continue the seeking
with a growing acceptance
after all these years
that the answers are both
deeply and truly known
yet always and forever
a mystery.

The Unkempt Man

How many times have I
averted my eyes from the unkempt man,
walked quickly by
hands tight in my pockets?
Remembering tales, I've told myself,
He'll just buy a bottle, or
The little I give won't make a difference.
I've voted for social programs,
donated to food banks.
I do my part, I say.
It is the truly wealthy
who should pay their share,
fund programs, provide jobs.

But, who am I to judge?
What right have I to choose
whether the unkempt man should
have food or the comfort of booze?

What I know is
I have more than enough
and he has less.
My bank account may be modest,
but, I am the truly wealthy,
with love and visions of peace
to go along with my full belly
and these coins in my pocket.

BECOMING THE CRONE

I've had enough birthdays that only
    the ones with zeros seem worth noting anymore.
Turning fifty was something—half a century!
So many personal dreams already fulfilled,
    and so much life ahead.
One hundred seemed suddenly—
    not necessary, but doable.
Sixty was fun, yet middle-ish,
    but seventy . . . aahhh . . . seventy!
I've over a year to go, but
    like the eleven-year-old-going-on-thirteen,
    or nineteen-going-on-twenty-one,
I already feel an excitement about seventy,
    a sense of accomplishment.
    No hemming and hawing,
    I'll definitely be senior.
I think it may take eighty to be an elder,
    but at seventy I'll claim crone.
And here's what I find so exciting—
    I'm so damned alive!
I walk with a good strong stride
    and I'm not giving it up.
The sight of the moon, a stunning sunset,
    or a new green shoot poking through the earth,
    still gives me a thrill.
Walking in the wind
    my arms can suddenly fly up in joy,
    spin me around, make me giggle.
A new idea, or an old one in a new light,
    still ignites a fire in me that burns as hot as ever.
I am rich with years of experience,
    a vibrant background in which to weave
    the new with a depth of understanding
    not possible at earlier turnings.

I can look back on accomplishments and,
       with the arms of a grandchild around my neck,
ahead at possibilities,
       while savoring the sweetness of now.
I know my place
       and know that at the heart of all knowing
       is still the mystery,
       still the wondering.
And I know that
       in the heart of the crone
       the child will always dance.

FOR MY DAUGHTERS

I had such dreams for you,
my baby girls,
as I touched my cheek
to your small heads nestled on my shoulder,
breathed in your sweet baby breath.
I would change the world for you,
clear the way for your growth
into full-powered women.
But it wasn't that easy, was it?
The world still harbors many problems,
so many things I would have changed.
Your fight, as you raise your own young ones,
is as great, perhaps greater than mine,
but, oh, my girls, my babes into women,
you are doing it so well.

Being Love

OH, RAVEN

I hear you call
as I light my candle this morning.
The flame seems so small,
my heart so heavy,
not nearly large enough
to hold so many woundings,
so many dear ones caught in pain.
My small flame burns
calling in Quan Yin,
calling in the larger hearts
calling in …

What's that you say, Raven?
Ah, of course, you are right.
The need is not for calling in.
It is for expanding out ...
    opening.
Love is always large enough
    to hold it all.

JUST WAITING FOR LOVE?

What is this?
Is love something to wait for?
Something to seek?
I think not.
No!
Love is something to do!
Something to be!
Love is mine.
Anytime, all the time.
I have only to open my heart
and let it pour
on
everything!

Always

Even when we do not notice,
    it is there,
calling in the laugh of a child
    the whisper of trembling leaves
    in birdsong,
beckoning us with a look
    in the eye of a friend
    or a pet,
the sight of the sunset,
    the still reflection on a lake,
drifting in on the scent
    of the sweet pea,
    a ripe peach,
    or rain-freshened earth,
caressing us with a breeze
    or the warmth of the sun
    on a cheek,
moving us to dance,
    to leap,
    to spin in circles of joy,
nudging us to open,
    to be,
    to fully embrace the love
that is always ready
    to be born.

Take Joy

Take that one tiny instant
the blush of color on the cloud
the sight of a lone calla
against the deep green of the woods
the sweet laughter of a child
the note of the singing bowl
take that one tiny instant of joy—
hold it tenderly in your heart
        your hands
rock it in your arms
smother it with kisses
until it explodes
into a thousand pieces
and fills the universe
with its own honeyed seedlings
to take root in other hearts
        other hands
to be caressed and rocked
and smothered again
with kisses.

Message

This morning
the universe gives me a message
for a loved one on a quest for happiness.
Oh how right it feels
if only she could hear me,
but I am the wrong messenger I fear.
My messages get filtered through pain
emerge as judgments
her own thoughts so intermingled with mine.
So maybe I can send this thought silently
and maybe she will hear it as her own.

HOLDING THE CENTER

The universe sings a song of change.
Some hearts race in panic
beating out the sound of doom
apocalypse, armageddon.
Be calm my heart.
Be filled with love, with light, compassion.
Join the steady beat of hearts
keeping time with the true song
the true hymn of the universe
the song of love, of joy.

Hold this.

Hold this.

I LOVE

…that in January
the peas in my garden are blooming
and the volunteer calendulas glow yellow and orange.
I love the roar of the surf,
the sunset light on the trunks of the cypress.
I love the smile that greets me each morning,
and the goodnight kisses, and the steady way
he keeps the fire burning to warm our house.
I love an afternoon chat with a friend,
staying in touch through life changes,
searching for meaning,
reading poetry, knitting socks.
I love the thought that my joyful heart
may absorb some small part of the heartache
of one I do not even know,
that a tiny sliver of my loving
may slip in to ease the universal pain.

TODAY

I must love my fellow humans
even the congressmen,
the deniers, nay sayers.

Today I must love
even the saber rattlers,
bomb throwers,
wall builders.

Today I must be large enough
to hold the earth,
to wrap the earth
in a blanket of peace.

Today I must write a poem,
light a candle,
be the light.

Today, right now in this moment,
I must glow.

NO JEWELS NEEDED

Given all that
nature provides,
the fruits to bloom
in your cheeks,
the stars
to light your eyes,
what need is there
for more adornment
than a smile?

Turning Up the Volume

Sometimes the news
or the list of onerous chores
gives me a pain
in the pit of my stomach
makes my head too heavy to hold
drowns out the secret hum
inside.

So, I walk under trees
stretching so high overhead,
breathe in the colors of sunset
drifting wisps of wonder,
hear my granddaughter's laugh
unfettered and free,
touch the hand of my dearest friend
always and forever there,
wrap myself
in the warmth of connection
with so many friends on this path,
known and unknown,
tuning in and turning up
the volume on that secret hum
    hum
      hum
        humming.

As I do these everyday things,
knowing that life
    at its very core
        is always
      good.

Joyful Presence

In this moment
my thoughts
could go up
or down
dragging my gullible
emotions along.
Now why
would I choose down,
when if I stay
in this moment,
alive and awake,
knowing that down
is nothing more
than opportunity
for up,
joy is so easy?

The Divine is in the Union

The blossom is sweet,
with its stamen
and its pistil,
masculine and feminine,
sweet enough to lure the bee
spread the pollen to the ovum,
produce the ultimate sweetness,
—ripened fruit,
succulent and nourishing,
neither masculine
nor feminine—
simply Divine.

Joy Shows Up

Joy shows up in a swath of daisies
a wagging tail when I reach for my walking shoes
the voice of a friend in an unexpected call
the smell of the rose bush as I brush by
the glowing color of the ripe raspberry
the burst of sweet tartness on my tongue
the satisfaction of a freshly cleaned room,
a job well done
clean sheets.

Joy shows up in smiles—
all smiles, smiles of loved ones,
strangers, old folks, and babies.

Joy shows up
as a picture of my grandchild in the morning's email
in a candle flame
a pretty stone
sun glowing through a leaf
birdsong
the play of light and shadow in the woods
flowing water, crystal clear in a trickling stream
a quiet moment
a good meal, fresh and tasty, shared with someone dear
warm eyes
a loving glance.

Joy shows up whenever I
show up
heart open
a willing receptacle
filled to overflowing
with the ever present
abundance.

The Preparation

In a long ago April,
my heart heavy from the winter's
dreams dashed and promises broken,
I took my young daughters
to play beside the river.
As they laughed and made up games,
I sat, my eyes drawn into the flow.
Mesmerized by the waters,
the heaviness in me melted away,
melted as the snows that fed the swollen river,
washed and cleansed
and filled with a contentment
that lifted my feet right off the ground,
so happy in my own company
that I nearly skipped the party that night,
but because a friend expected me
I floated through the door
and into the eyes
of the one who would be my life partner.
Love is like that
coming only when we make ourselves ready.

Unconditional Love

It is not that you
are everything
I need you to be.
It's just that you are

and that is all
I need.

DARKTIME

Going down
deep into the place
before belonging
the place of waiting
wanting
if I were to lose you
if I were to lose you
how could I wait
for another spring.

Give me your hand
bring me back into this moment
breathe into this moment
all the joy that has been
all the joy that will be
as we remember the seeds
new seeds always
waiting in the darkness
to be born.

THE WELL

We can always reach deep
and find as much as is needed,
but sometimes the well
must be refilled with tears.

TIME OUT OF TIME

In that magic
head-over-heels time of new love
when we'd been with one another
enough to know for sure
how good we were together
we began to wonder
could we still be alone?

So…
one night
you stayed in your mountain cabin
and me in my valley apartment
each of us in our own company,
doing our own business,
finding our own pleasures.

I chose a bath by candlelight
watching the light play and the water
rise and fall with my breath
soaking, savoring
content
and just as I got out
there you were at my door.

A fine evening, you said,
and feeling good
you thought you'd take a drive
and if by chance my light was still on…

I was not sorry to see you.
We knew what we needed to know.
Each of us was whole alone,
strong, true, sure of our core
but together
ah, together…
we made such
sweet fire.

I Still See It

still see the magic of that sweet baby girl
enchanted by fairies
blessed by the smiling moon
born of a love so tender and fierce
in my own young and innocent heart.

I saw it in the child with scabby knees
and scraggly hair
in the defiant teen
bursting with her own eagerness to bloom,
saw it in the new mother struggling
with parenting issues of her own.

I see it in the woman, now in her early forties,
bruised by life's challenges
angry and in pain
still see the magic
the enchantment in this being
whom I love with the same fierceness
as when I first held my sweet small babe.

If only…if only…
I could hold the mirror
in just the right position
that she might see it, too.

To My Pregnant Daughter

We lived nine months as one
and then, days after I first held you in my arms,
we lay, your tiny newborn form on mine,
and in that instant between wakefulness
and sleep as I felt you relax onto my chest,
for a fleeting moment I sensed
the tiny body as my own.
I was you,
the tiny one
the miracle,
the oneness of us
sending my heart to the moon.
From that sweet moment on
my job was to be the one
who let you be you.

Now here you are,
your own belly swelling with new life,
and the connection comes back
with a fierceness
that makes me shudder in delight,
a connection that goes back through me
to my mother and grandmothers
and forward through you to your child
and your children's children,
connected through our amazing life giving,
life sustaining womanly bodies
with the precious gift of giving and receiving.
Oh the wonder, the magic,
the sheer joy of it!

BORN UNDER A PERSEID METEOR SHOWER

At the foot of Mount Shasta
the boy lay on his lawn
and in stillness
sensed the spinning of the earth
as overhead uncountable pinpoints of sparkling light—
stars-planets-galaxies—
arced across the midnight sky.
His mother lay in her sleeping bag beside him,
their only tent the canopy of stars.
At ten he spent three months
walking in circles to the "Unchained Melody"
grinding the lens for his own telescope
that he might get a bit closer to the magic.
As a man he roused his sleepy daughters
and took them to the nearest, highest, clearest points
that they might share with him some celestial event.
For years he gave star talks
to the hundreds who made the trek
away from the lights of town
to see the vision that stirred him so.
He does not speak much of spirit but
never misses an opportunity to gaze at the heavens
and each year the cosmos celebrates
the anniversary of his birth
with a grand display of shooting stars.

IN PRAISE OF HANDS

I think of my hands
kneading bread
folding laundry
caressing babies
washing dishes
stitching quilts
and clothing and toys,
taking the dictation
from my mind and heart
stories and poems,
drawing, painting, stitching
the story images,
hands that dig into the earth
reach up in praise and gratitude,
follow the teachings
and patterns of my ancestors,
forge new paths,
new ways, new teachings
for my generation
and those to come,
hands that will not
lead me astray
as long as they stay
so closely connected
to my heart.

Disillusioned

Illusion.
Disillusion.
Which is which?
I could say my disillusion came with years
of seeing one war follow another war,
changes in education going,
to my mind, backward instead of forward,
chest beating and bickering unending.
With my children having children
I wondered where was that better world
I was so sure I would create for them?

But maybe the illusion is in the politics,
the wars, false struggles for meaning,
and to be disillusioned is to see
that the secret…the truth…lies
in keeping at the fore the awareness
that the sun rises and sets every day,
often in splendid show,
rains refresh,
seeds sprout and blossom,
children raised in love grow
strong and healthy,
compassion matters,
love is at the core of everything,
and life…real life…
is always good.

Helium for the Heart

I closed the book just as
my two-year-old woke from her nap.
Touching my tears she asked,
"Why are you crying?"
"I was reading a sad story," I told her.
She opened the book
and held it up for me to see,
"Don't cry, Mama. It's not sad.
See? It's just ABCs."

Just ABCs.
Just protons and particles.
It's not sad. It's story.
Heartbreaking, weary-making,
life-destroying story,
unless I breathe deep.
Breathe in love.
Breathe out compassion.
Breathe in caring.
Breathe out love.
Breathe deeply
and that same heavy, broken heart
expands, lifts, floats,
encompassing all,
weighing nothing,
like a balloon filled with helium.

Does it strike you as odd that the
caring that makes the heart so heavy
is the same caring that makes it light?
The difference between my heart
and the helium balloon is that
with the balloon
it is taking in that lifts it,
but with my heart
it is breathing out the love
that gives it wings.

Some Days

Some days the gloom pulls hard.
The inviting shroud lures me
to curl up and hide,
rock myself in the dark and cry.
Too hard, too hard, all this bickering,
lies held as truths
no reason can unclench,
fear and greed rampant,
compassion not nearly enough.
Step into the light,
the poet says,
step and face and lift your eyes,
so I step in spite of the gloomy clouds,
step out and see the bright calendulas,
golden and glowing,
holding the power of the sun.
Look and listen, the poet says,
even the dark iris whisper promises,
soon there will be raspberries.

First Hand

My aunt bought the fabric
for the dresses
that my mother sewed
for my cousin to wear one year
and me the next
so I never got to choose
the patterns or the colors,
but I didn't mind.
I was just happy
that it was my mom
who knew how to sew.

TRENCH FOR THE PHONE LINE

I'd rather be writing poetry, but
we have this bothersome trench to dig.
Where, I wonder, is the joy in that?
Cold seeps deep into my leg bones
as I kneel and plunge my trowel
into the root riddled earth.
Eighteen inches is a long way down,
seventy feet a lot of distance to cover.
At least it isn't raining.
There is some joy in that, I suppose.

My muscles quiver as I lift the pick
for what feels like the hundredth time,
though it can't have been more than twenty.
My husband, grumbler, doubter, awfulizer,
mutters, "We'll never get under this pipe.
It's impossible."
"Let me work on that," I say.
"You do the heavy digging."
I'm good at the impossible,
getting a job done against the odds.
He swings the pick with a force
I can't muster. We dig on.

The warm sun feels good on my back.
I apologize to the redwood roots,
the worms and grubs, to Mother Earth herself,
noticing how the sun lights the colors
of her soil, thinking how it is the sun
that grows the plants, that rot to become
the dark humus, that grows more plants.
Light to dark to light to dark to light.
Earth and sun united in this rich black soil.
I'm digging sunlight. I enjoy the thought.

My husband calls, "I think this is going to work."
His smile, as always, warms my heart.
We do work well together,
me with the faith and him the strength.
We'll finish the job, then sip hot cocoa
and congratulate one another
on yet another accomplishment.
There's the joy — in relationship,
in the earth, the sun, a job well done,
and, now, another poem.

YOU ASK THE SOURCE OF MY JOY

Oh, this is an easy question.
One with many answers.
At this moment I might say
it is the glow
of the floating clouds
changing now from rose to gold,
or the redwoods standing
tall and strong
against the dawning sky,
or the soft light whispering
to the greening earth,
"Wake up, wake up, my sweet.
It's morning."

Ask me at noon, or dusk
and the answer would be different,
but always,
always it would include
the light in your eyes,
your smile,
the way you are always
so happy to see me.

SACRED WOUNDINGS

A dear one plunges into the dark night of the soul,
mired in the muck of past wrongs,
dredging through the pain of former losses,
accusations,
recriminations,
reproaches,
… at others
… at herself
She plunges the knife deepest into her own heart
again and again,
… and again.

I love you,
I call out across the chasm.
I love you.
I have always loved you.
I am sorry for the times
I failed you,
sorry for my part in any pain you feel or ever felt
or ever will feel,
sorry for the times I could not control my own horse
and left you to fend for yourself on the path.

Do I say, please forgive me?
It does not matter for me whether you do or not.
It matters for you.
It matters for you that you forgive all those wrongs.
It matters most of all that you forgive yourself
for feeling that you must have somehow deserved them.
You don't. You didn't.
You were a little girl, a woman learning about life.
We are all of us a mixture of past mistakes,
past hurts and joys and loves and losses,
and it is all right.
All of it is all right.

It is just what it is,
a matter of perception.
Illusion. Not real.
Everything and nothing.
It all comes down to this,
love yourself
and know that you are loved
for you are a precious part of the divine
and you are my child.

To My Sister

Remember when I got hurt
falling through the rail
on the basement stairs
and my head bled all over my shirt
and they put me in Grandma's bed to rest?

We were always at odds, you and I,
even when we were small,
you so stubborn,
you'd always have your way,
and me with my temper.

But that day
when Grandma brought you in
to see me lying there,
I saw something in your eyes,
a concern that surprised me
went straight to my heart,
and in that one magic moment
everything was all right.

After the Heart Attack

The time for gestation passed and still
the child lingered in the womb
until the father dreamed
of an empty blue bunting and knew
that to accept this beloved into his life
he must also accept the possibility of loss.
Point and counterpoint.

Oh, my beloved, I knew
as our love grew and blossomed to fullness
that one day the rose petals would begin to fall,
one by one or all at once,
but not so soon, not yet.
We protected ourselves, didn't we?
…with lifestyle choices to keep us strong?
I know nothing is for sure,
nothing is forever,
but for a long, long time
for all the time fore-seeable…
at least that long.

We find ourselves, now, face to face
with the truth that the moment of vulnerability
is not someday.
It is now. It is here
where we stand in this precious moment
each heart within the other singing.

HOLDING

"Letting go is always easier than holding on,"
so said my message from the Universe
the day after we got news of my mother's
deteriorating heart.
Is it time for letting go?
Or time yet for holding on?
Easier for the one leaving,
or the ones left behind?

Our family dog, when left alone
would go into each room and collect
one item from each of us—a slipper,
a dirty sock, a favorite scarf, a teddy bear—
then sit with his pile of comforts until our return.

Today in this time of uncertainty
I gather comforts around me—
messages from my children and siblings,
the vase Mom sent home with me,
a constant in her home since before I can remember,
the voices of my friends lifting one another,
poetry—sweet joyful poetry,
the sun winking at me through the redwood branches,
the lily pads floating on the pond in the morning stillness,
Gary in the kitchen making waffles just because.

Surrounded by these and more I wait for news,
believing this time, it won't be too bad,
there will be more time, more visits,
knowing that one day,
maybe sooner than I had expected,
certainly sooner than I want,
it will be the time for letting go
and even then, even as I let go,
I — we — will be held by love.

LETTERS

February 3, 2014
Moving day, a sweet girl writes
a love letter to the only home she's ever known.
"Dear, Dear 512,
I will miss you sooo very, very much.
Thank you for the awesome adventures."
She adds a PS: "For whoever finds this note,
make another for this house and put it here."
She tucks her note into a cupboard
and closes the door.

April 19, 1944
From his base in Britain a young flyer
writes to his sister back home,
"So you've fallen for a navigator? That's
what you get when you fall for a navigator."

August 11, 1944
A navigator writes to his folks
from the prison camp hospital,
"I had the misfortune to pick up a wound.
I am healing. I am okay. Tell Ruth
I still feel the same about her.
They only let me write to you."

May 19, 1945
He writes to his girl,
"I am a free man again. Some
of the fellows had it rather rough,
but it wasn't so bad for me.
I had plenty to eat if you like
potatoes and brown bread.
Remember I love you My Darling."

Letters.
Markers in time,
tucked away in cupboards
and keepsake boxes,
saved by mothers and lovers
so "whoever finds this" will know…
love was here.

IN THE MOMENT

I watch the dancing
colors in the garden,
read the sweet poem
from my granddaughter
look into the gentle eyes
of my partner
of thirty-five years
and in each case
the love I feel
exploding in my heart
is for the whole world.

TRIMMING THE TREE

Crawling into the back of the closet
I fight a mental reluctance;
so much work for a few days that will fly too quickly by.
Then it will all have to be put away again. More work.
We bring in the ladders, wrestle with strings of lights.
It's not so easy for us now
without the excited squeals of the young ones to spur us on.
Just the two of us . . . for how many years now?
. . . a dozen? . . . more?
The way it is, the way it's supposed to be
when the children have grown, have families of their own.
You put on the Christmas music and as I open the boxes,
the flood of memories washes away any resistance,
any hesitation to be fully engaged.

Here are the walnuts with red yarn from Bethany's first tree,
snowflakes crocheted by my mother,
the eggshells the kids and I painted one year,
only three left now—I handle them with extra care—
shiny pieces from Grandma Hines,
lots of angels, hearts, and doves,
speaking to me as always of the true spirit,
the tin icicles we got on our trip to Vermont,
and the hand-blown glass ones from the little shop
just down the street from our home in Milford.
Here's the big red jingle bell from Jacob's first Christmas—
place it low where Linnea can see it this year—
and these with pictures of Emmett and Violet,
remember how she always hung upside down like that?
Hand-made ornaments, gifts from friends;
we hang each treasure carefully, seeking balance, harmony.

Then satisfied and weary we lie on the floor to stretch our backs,
looking forward, looking back
while being in this perfect moment.
I snuggle into the crook of your arm and kiss you.
"This," you say, "is the true meaning of life."

January Second

My children have gone to their own homes
leaving me with gifts of a temple bell
and a garden Buddha.

Under the Christmas tree which
still glows for us in the evenings
even though its time has past,
Buddha waits, quietly overlooking
their childhood village,
needle-pointed so many years ago.
Perhaps today he'll move
to his intended spot by the pond
where I'll see him as I look out each morning,
and the bell will be hung in the entry window
to be rung in the Thai tradition
upon entering our temple home.

This morning I sit wrapped in this rich tapestry of love,
contemplating what has been, what is, what will be;
past.... present... future... earthly and spiritual.
Can you hear my heart humming?

Post Holiday Lament

Holidays over
last hugs hugged and hugged again
seven days ago.
Leftovers eaten,
tree down, ornaments stowed,
all over and done.

But under the table,
a pair of fuzzy slippers,
o-eyes tufted ears,
peering out, they wait.
Let them stay, my heart whispers,
maybe she's still here.

TIME TO CALL ON LOVE

Clouds
trap the sun today,
dark and heavy.
Hungry children
will go unfed
because the powerful
stir trepidation in the gut
of the hard working,
create a haze of fear
overshadowing fairness
justice, compassion,
in those who,
in times of disaster,
dig deep to help,
those whose hearts are good,
causing them to join the chorus,
"Don't take money from the rich.
They've earned it!
They deserve to keep it."

High above the haze,
the sun remains,
above the clouds of fear.
It's time to unleash God,
burn through those clouds,
let the power shine
from above,
from within,
fiery and passionate,
burn through the fears
to reveal our true nature…
love…
        simply love.

FOR ETERNITY

When I am gone from this physical earth
I want no markers left behind,
no monuments or shrines,
save perhaps a stepping stone
to help those who come after.
Let any space I've occupied
be left open, renewed,
rejuvenated by future generations.
Should my words be remembered
let it be because of the hearts they touch.
I've no need for immortality
and if there is a place
where my name is written
for eternity by some divine pen
let it be this . . .

                  Love.

Connection
and
Change

MAY DAY TAKE TWO

May first, May Day!
I move the clothes rack
from its indoor winter spot
and hang my wash
to dry in the sunshine.
May Day! It's spring.
It's really spring!
My heart hums with the bees
buzzing in the raspberry blossoms,
sings with the birds.
May Day! May Day!
A time for celebration,
for dancing 'round Maypoles
and gathering nosegays.
May Day! May Day!

Another refrain, deeper down.
Same words, different sound,
a cry for help.
Mayday-mayday-mayday!
A call from the earth,
from the barren rainforests,
the melting icecaps,
the intensified storms.
Mayday-mayday-mayday!
A desperate cry.

My heart hears both.
May Day! May Day!
A song of joy.
It's spring! It's spring!
May Day! May Day!
Go ahead, sing the song,
live in the joy,
but hang the wash
and don't forget.
Mayday-mayday-mayday!
don't forget, don't forget.

HARMONICS

I vibrate with a frequency
that cannot be heard,
a light that cannot yet
be seen by all.
I am not alone.
there are thousands of us
holding the frequency,
holding the center;
tens of thousands,
hundreds of thousands,
vibrating, shining
with all our might
with all our being.
Each night I watch
the evening news for a sign
but hear only of disasters,
of wars, economic strife,
political maneuvering,
a crying earth.
One day though,
one day soon,
there will be enough of us
vibrating, singing,
shining our light
that when we are joined
by just one more,
one more being vibrating
at this harmonious frequency,
it will be enough
that the whole world
will see and hear
and the universe itself
will ring out
in glorious celebration.

LABOR PAINS

Rumblings in the earth,
stirrings in the weather patterns;
hurricanes, tornadoes,
hottest years,
coldest years,
devastating floods.
Leaders gridlocked,
blind selfish greed running rampant,
widening the chasm between
haves and have-nots
to an unleapable size.
Oppressed people rising,
discontent stirring,
rumbling, roaring,
taking to the streets.

One might wish
for a simpler time,
a quieter time,
pastoral days watching
fluffy clouds floating in fields of blue.
One might moan and writhe
crying, *Doom! Doom! Doom!*

Or one might sense
in the darkness and disruption
the excitement of change,
the emergence of the new.
One might,
instead of moaning and writhing,
choose to dance, to sing,
to love, to embrace,
to breathe through these labor pangs,
knowing that the new
the bright
the ecstatic
is being born.

Natural High

My antennae are out
madly waving
sending signals
high frequencies of joy
receiving signals in return
stimulating responses
joy scattering
attracting joy
thoughts breeding
more thoughts
from me
to me
a sense of wonder
of possibility
making connections
seen and unseen
smiles contagious
ideas springing
from the fertile universe
blossoming
their fragrance
wafting to other noses
emerging as song
voices joined
the dance begins
of infinity
of possibility!

OPENING THE DOORS

Sitting on my cushion, eyes closed
my heart-mind easily expands
sending love to all the universe.
Looking out at the sunset colors in my garden
my spirit sings love songs
as ecstatic as those of Rumi.
Thinking of so many people
with whom my connection is strong
my heart overflows with joy and wonder,
for those in need the compassion pours easily.

But let me see a headline on Time magazine
about children needing more schooling
instead of vacation time at the beach,
or hear the news anchor giving war reports,
or see the face of the Congressman
arguing that we cannot afford to take care
of the needs of the unemployed
while he votes to fund the endless war
and protect the interests of oil companies
at the expense of our life sustaining earth,
and something within me flares.
Doors in my heart slam shut!

It is not so easy to love those
whom I see as greedy or short-sighted,
the ones who do not yet see
the need for peace, for compassion,
protection of our sacred earth.
And so today I pray, please let me
open those doors in my heart.
Let me love these beings, too,
without condition, without hesitation,
with compassion as sincere as that
which I extend to my dear ones,
to those who suffer at their hands.

Let me not see greed and stupidity,
but human beings, sentient beings.
Let me see their human faces as I look
upon the lovely colors in my garden
expand my heart to take in all the universe
For if I am truly one with all,
my heart can have no doors.

Have You Heard?

Did you hear?
The dragon of change has opened her eyes!
Oh croon to her, you singers,
welcome her awakening with sweet melodic voice.
Massage her waking limbs, oh healers,
gently set them tingling that she may rise.
Pray for her, believers,
let your faith give fire to her breath,
and you, dear poets, write sonnets to her,
love ditties in her praise.
Gardeners, bring your fruits and flowers,
festoon her with garlands and set out the feast,
Gather round, gather round
for surely you've heard…
the dragon of change has opened her eyes.
Dress in your finest, bring out your best,
give all of your gifts
and let's start the dance.

CRASH AND BURN

Is this economy going down in flames
and if so, is that a bad thing?
This endless more, more, more of things,
cycles of producing,
using resources,
overflowing landfills with stuff
that is only useful for a season,
made just to keep the spiral
of production and consumption
moving ever upward.

Wasn't it inevitable that it would someday
crash and burn?
Should we be surprised,
try to prop it up for another round,
or let it fall,
making way for something new,
something where we set our sights
on more than making product,
where survival isn't based
on having more,
but on having enough,
on sharing,
on caring,
on being?
Where creations are connected
more to the heart than to the purse,
deeper, richer, filled with joy?

Give me the strength to help those
whom this change
pushes to the edge of nothing,
those who don't have the essentials
of physical survival,
but if this is the change
that will allow the emergence
of the new story ...

Oh, let it come!
Sing it, write it, paint it,
plant it, praise it,
welcome it
into being!

Cosmic Hatching

To be alive today
is to know there is a crack in the cosmic egg,
to know something more-than-new
pecks and pushes its way into our consciousness.
To be alive today is to open our hearts,
blessing those who tremble and retreat
as the old dies and re-manifests a new form.
To be alive today
is to dance the rites of fertility
calling the new to emerge
as the old crumbles around us,
to hold our hands in a sacred circle
and chant the *om* in the birthing chamber.
To be alive today is to raise our voices
singing out in joyful celebration.
To be alive today is to be *alive!*

HEART SIGNALS

(best read aloud)

The heart
sends signals
good vibes
bad vibes
ten feet
at least
so if
I'm in
your zone
I catch
your vibes
between
we two
we reach
twenty feet
and if
we send
good vibes
we might
touch him
and her
and them
and then
we'd beat
in sync
and catch
up more
and more
and more
and if
someone
got in
whose vibes
rang fear
not love

we'd wrap
her up
in all
our love
and ease
that fear
with our
good vibes
how cool!

Flip Side of the Numbers Game

Sometimes
the numbers don't add up.
They are manipulated,
skewed to prove the point,
stir the fears of one side
or the other.
Then the only thing to do
is go to what my heart knows best,
this simple truth;
no matter how you add it up,
subtract, multiply, or divide,
no matter how you draw
the graphs and pie charts,
the answer in the end
is always
One.

THINKING SCIENTIFICALLY

Live DNA in a beaker
three-hundred-fifty miles from its source
responds to the emotions of its donor.
Once connected, always connected.
Imagine that!

The heart radiates electromagnetic energy,
measured up to ten feet away,
five thousand times more powerful
than the energy of the brain.
Imagine that!

As few as one hundred people
creating peace within themselves
reduced crime and violence
in their cities of ten thousand.
Imagine that!

Love creates a coherence in our world,
negative emotions cause disharmony.
We, with our strong hearts, are in control.
Scientists have measured, tested,
calculated these effects and say as few
as eight thousand in a world of six billion
are enough to start the change.
Imagine that!

Now imagine seven thousand nine-hundred
ninety-eight people, along with you and me,
all of us filling our powerful hearts
with thoughts of love and peace,
imagining a world without war, terror, or crime,
without cancer, HIV, heart disease, or hunger,
a world where air and water are pure and clean,
where every child is wanted, every person knows
that he or she is loved—is love itself.
Just imagine that!

READ ME A POEM

The news keeps coming
disaster on top of disaster
fears run amuck
and I stand at this threshold
agitated, disturbed
seeking a vision
a calm space to hold.
I read words about laughter,
about joy erupting,
but in this moment
joy eludes me
and I remember
putting a fevered child into a bath
in the middle of the night
sponging her with cool water.
"Read me a poem," she says.
Poems had seen us through
teething, tummy aches,
two-year-old tantrums.
Now in her fever she begs,
"Read me a poem, Mama."
And so I hold the big blue book
and read and sponge,
sponge and read,
until at last we cross
the threshold to sleep and health.
As I stand now
on this new threshold
in my own feverish state
I plead,
"Read me a poem, Mama.
Oh, Great Mama,
please, read me a poem."

SPRING HILL

I sit in silence at the headwaters
watching water flow from crevices in the rocks,
flow crystal clear and pure across the stones,
then plunge in a bubbling white froth
down over the falls and onward.
I sit in silence and think of all the lives
this water will touch,
all the beings—plant and animal—
along its way,
spring becoming stream,
then river,
joining with other waters,
making its way
through the mountains,
across the great valley
and into the great Pacific sea.

I sit in silence and think of you—all of us—
whose light flows
from the deep crevices of our being,
light flowing into streams of crystal clarity,
bubbling into frothy laughter,
connecting and touching and lighting the way,
with our words,
with our thoughts,
with our love,
our connection magnifying the glow
that other lights may be kindled,
headwaters of a new way
a new vision from an ancient wisdom
a new world of love and laughter,
clarity and light.

Please Pass the Kindness

In a world of adrenalin junkies
when the back-of-the-hand to everything
surrounds us in our non-stop news cycle,
in our entertainment,
in our response to any wrong or perceived wrong,
where one murder is no longer enough
to keep the excitement pumped in a whodunit,
where the deaths of three thousand
extend to a decade of untallied
widows, orphans, grieving parents,
young men and women maimed and broken,
an exponential expansion of those who perceive us as enemy,
a citizenry shaking in their boots and clinging to their guns
in a fear-ridden, fear-driven world,
some of us—
more and more and more of us—
know that strength is not more back-of-the-hand retaliation,
that neither honor nor healing is gained by revenge,
that release is not to be found in ever more adrenalin,
but
in silence
in kindness
in nature
in companionship and compassion
in listening
in nourishing the budding of the new shoots.

ENTELECHY

It is loud within the womb
rumblings of transition,
transformation,
the rhythmic breathing,
heart beating,
sustaining us as we morph
into what will be.
Have we been
for these millennia,
in a larval stage,
a great caterpillar
devouring, growing
preparing for this time?

Are we in a womb
or a cocoon?
Morphing through
the stages of our ontogeny
from zygote to fetus,
or a mush,
letting go of all we've been
to be reborn into
some entirely new form,
caterpillar to butterfly.

It is loud in here
and not always pleasant,
but this I know
the seed, the plan,
the desire to be,
whatever it is we are to be,
is strong within us
and will not be denied.
Already it beats
with a joy-filled
heart of its own.

My Ho'oponopono Prayer

For those times I have allowed myself
to languish in the mediocre
hesitant to hurt too much
or shine too brightly
or been too long stuck in the dark
failing to accept and acknowledge
the depth of its teachings
and thereby not contributed
my best efforts for the greater good
I am truly sorry.
Please forgive me.

For the richness of that darkness
the iridescence of the colors
revealed only in the depths
for the brilliant insights
creative passions
love and deep compassion
that spring from the dark
in dazzling contrast
illuminating, glowing,
growing our universe

and for the everyday
transitional times
that weave it all together
connecting dark and light
and you and me
in the great tapestry
wrapping us in love
that we may
each of us
and all of us
be what we are meant to be,
I am so inexpressibly grateful.

I thank you
and I love you.

NOT TO BRAG

...but I bear the babies
stir the soup pot
tend the garden
keep the fire burning on the hearth.

I sing the lullabies
tell the stories
give words to the
heartbeat of the earth.

I dye the wool
spin the yarn
knit booties and shawls
weave tapestries
give vision to the dreams.

I hold sacred the past
keep an eye to the future
seven generations on.
One ear turns outward
to the music of the spheres
the other leans down to catch
the whispers of a child.

I am one of many
who are One
holder of the hearts
seeker of the wisdom
bearer of the pains and joys
grower of the wings
that one day all may fly.

ON THE NETWORKS

We sit down to the news on PBS,
another night, like the other nights.
My partner says
"Can't they find something different to say?"
Where is the news of the miracle
of peace spreading heart to heart,
group to group,
of the power of the morning call,
of the singing children,
the poets, storytellers, painters
birthing the new story?
"Seek and ye shall find."
"Build it and they will come."

If I ruled the world
there would be not just
a news flash interrupting,
but a whole station,
a world-wide network
devoted to the good news,
spreading joy and peace and love
like a blanket,
quenching the flames of destruction.
Who would not tune in?
Who would not rise to share,
join, expand, magnify?
Tune in seekers,
tune in and let's all
broadcast loud and clear.
They will hear.
We will hear.
Love, peace, joy
will ring in every ear.

LONG DIVISION

Hemispheres
Quadrants
Continents
Countries
East
West
North
South
Us
Them
So many ways to divide
to forget it is
One.
Earth.

Declaration

We
the One
will change
the world.

www.ingramcontent.com/pod-product-compliance
Lightning Source LLC
Chambersburg PA
CBHW031844090426

42741CB00005B/343